SOUTHERN FRONTIERSMAN

THE
STORY
OF
GENERAL
SAM
DALE

BY THE SAME AUTHOR

REBEL SEA RAIDER
The Story of Raphael Semmes

GUADALCANAL GENERAL
The Story of A. A. Vandegrift USMC

SOUTHERN FRONTIERSMAN

THE STORY OF GENERAL SAM DALE

BY JOHN FOSTER

ILLUSTRATED BY LESLIE GRAY

C 3 Y

WILLIAM MORROW & COMPANY   NEW YORK 1967

FOR MY BROTHER GEORGE,
who used to tell me stories,
in hopes he would have liked
this true one.

CONTENTS

SOUTHERN FRONTIERSMAN

THE
STORY
OF
GENERAL
SAM
DALE

1

THE SOUTHERN FRONTIER

Baron Hector de Carondelet, Spanish governor of Louisiana, cast an apprehensive eye toward the horde of restless Americans pressing upon the eastern boundaries of Spain's New World colony in the late eighteenth century. Reporting from his New Orleans headquarters, he wrote:

> A carbine and a little maize in a sack are enough for an American to wander about in the forests alone for a whole month. With his carbine he kills the wild cattle and deer for food and defends himself against the savages. The maize dampened serves him in lieu of bread. With some tree trunks crossed one above another, in the shape of a square, he raises a house, and even a fort, that is impregnable to the savages. . . .

Carondelet, who in 1792 signed a treaty arranging to give the Creek Indians arms and ammunition to wage war upon the white invaders, was describing the American pioneer in general. Unknowingly, he also had set down a highly accurate pen portrait of Sam Dale, the Southern frontiersman and redoubtable Indian fighter whom a nineteenth century historian called "the Daniel Boone of Alabama."

Dale had border fighting in the very marrow of his bones. On both his father's and mother's side he was Scotch-Irish. The Scotch-Irish were a rugged group of Presbyterians from the Lowlands of Scotland, who had been settled in Northern Ireland by English sovereigns early in the 1600's to promote loyalty in a rebellious land.

Toward the end of the century, annoyed by high taxation, religious restrictions, and additional curbs, these fiercely independent people began to leave Ireland for Pennsylvania and other frontier parts of America. Accustomed for generations to the grim border warfare of the Scottish Lowlands, the cutthroat troubles in Ireland, and the Indian fighting in America, the Scotch-Irish made the best possible frontiersmen.

Dale's parents both were born near Carlisle, in the south central part of Pennsylvania. Soon after their marriage, they moved with the great southward flood of German and Scotch-Irish pioneers to the border country in Rockbridge County, Virginia, on the eastern edge of the Appalachian Mountains. Samuel Dale, first of their nine children, was born in a one-room log cabin there in 1772.

The Dales and others of their ilk did not settle. They were always in the first wave moving into new territory. Clutching their deadly rifles and straight-handled axes, they came along with their light step and restless eyes, advancing like a skirmish line through the great, green, breathing forest that quickly swallowed them up. Wherever they sojourned, the forest wall surrounded them, ominous, full of wolves, bear, panthers, and hostile Indians. No man can resist his environment completely. The wilderness assaulted these men at the same time they were assaulting it, changed them even as they were changing it. In the dark, brooding gloom of the forest, the frontiersman became a different person, somewhat grimmer than before, more resolute, and stronger, ever stronger in mind and body.

On the border the individual was important, but the key to frontier life was cooperation—both within the family and outside it. Within the family, each person had his particular chores to perform. Also the constant threat of Indian attack made it necessary for families to combine, forming a co-op and building a stockade. Boys fell in love with and married girls they knew in the stockade, so that the families of the first wave were linked by ties of blood and loyalty much as the old clans in Scotland were.

Then, as others followed them into the territory, making it less dangerous, the first wave moved again, leaving with never a backward glance their little cabins in the stump-dotted yards, the scattered corn patches, and the stockades. They moved forward, thriving on peril and adversity, seeking ever greener grass, bluer skies, and fresh experiences, but more than anything else the exhilarating sensation of true and utter freedom. Such were the frontiersmen, the incredible, irrepressible people who unconsciously and even carelessly hacked out the destiny of their nation, a race of men the like of which no other country on earth has produced.

As the Baron de Carondelet had said, maize—Indian corn—was their staple. The frontiersmen could not have done what they did without Indian corn. This hardy cereal has been said to be the most important dietary discovery in the history of the South. It could be grown with little or no plowing. The frontiersmen ate it as roasting ears, as grits, hominy, and mush. Mixed with cold water and covered with hot ashes, it became the ashcake; put on a board and set near the hot coals, it became the journeycake, from which came johnnycake. Parched and ground, it made a meal in itself when mixed with water.

In 1775, when Dale was three, his parents moved once more with the advancing pioneers to the forks of the Clinch River in southwestern Virginia, part of the most exposed and turbulent of all American frontiers. There at Glade Hollow they threw up a stockade with some other families and stopped for a spell. In Glade Hollow Dale spent his early boyhood.

Like all successful frontiersmen, Dale devoted his formative years to getting a thorough education in the ways of the forest. He learned to identify sounds, how to find water, to track wild animals, to avoid poison oak and poison ivy, bees and wasps—as well as what to do when he hadn't been able to avoid them—how to build a fire in the rain, to make a "raccoon bridge" by felling a tree across a stream.

The ax was the frontiersman's most important tool, and in a pinch it served as an excellent weapon in the hand-to-hand combat that was so common along the border. During cold weather Dale heated the head to make it less brittle before using it and always smeared it with hog lard afterward to prevent rust.

His father taught him to shoot as soon as he was big enough to hold a rifle. The gun he used was the famous .40-caliber long rifle of the frontier, sometimes called the Pennsylvania rifle, sometimes the Kentucky rifle, and America's first real contribution to the design of firearms. With it a trained shot could put a ball into a man-sized target at three hundred yards—three times the effective range of a musket.

The secret of the great efficiency of the long rifle was in the method of loading. This procedure departed radically from the European custom of forcing down a naked lead ball the same size as the muzzle. The Americans used a smaller ball (seventy bullets from a pound of lead) and wrapped it in a patch of greased leather or cloth. The patch, which fitted tightly into the rifling grooves, cleaned the bore as it was being driven down. When the rifle was fired, the patch gave the ball its necessary spin, then fell off soon after the bullet left the muzzle. By the simple device of the patch, the old problem of the accumulation of fouling in a rifled weapon was solved.

The long rifle was the best weapon of its type in the world, but it took about thirty seconds to load. That period of relative helplessness was a vital factor in forest combat, allowing the Indians to press in before the rifleman could reload. Young Dale spent long hours trying to cut down on those thirty seconds, racing through the successive movements—pulling the stopper from the power horn with his teeth, ramming the patched ball down the barrel, priming the weapon —and then making sure he hit his target.

More diligently than anything else, however, the boy studied the Indian, learning his language, his stratagems, his strong points, his weaknesses. Of that period, a contemporary biographer later quoted Dale as saying, "It was a wild precarious life, often interrupted by ambuscade and massacre. But no one of that hardy frontier race was ever known to return to the settlements. Even the women and children became inured to peril, and cheerfully moved forward in this daring exodus to the West."

Glade Hollow was in the country of the Shawnee, since the Revolutionary War the most bellicose of all Indian nations. Dale's earliest recollections were of Shawnee attacks, finding the scalped corpses of neighbors and watching from the cabin floor as his mother stood guard at the bolted door with a rifle in her hands, an ax by her side.

To the Southern Indian, war was "the beloved occupation." Long before the white man came, the various nations fought among themselves constantly, not to conquer each other or to take over a neighboring tribe's territory, but to run great risks and to gather scalp trophies and loot. War was a game.

After the white man arrived, war continued to be the Indians' beloved occupation and a game, but now it took on a more practical nature. The red men were fighting for their ancestral home, for their very existence. Also the scalps were more colorful and the loot was infinitely more desirable. Everything the white man owned was highly prized, from horses to weapons to trinkets and women's clothing.

Of all the mysteries about these strange, hairy people with pale faces and knobby knees who came in their huge ships out of a sea that the Indians had thought was the end of the world, the greatest enigma was their solemn insistence upon legal ownership of the land. In the red man's belief, the Great Spirit had provided the land and stocked it with game for the good of his children. One could no more own the land than he could the air above it or the rain that fell upon it.

In the long, sad struggle between the two races, the red man never did grasp the white man's principle of land titles. The Indian fully realized, however, that both he and the white man wanted to live on the same land and that only one could have his way. And so the two races fought to the death.

The war waged in the cool gloom of the Southern forest was bitter, cruel to the extreme. No frontiersman could go to sleep any night without first facing the knowledge that tomorrow might be the last for him, his wife, his children. No man could return from a hunt free from the nagging dread that the next rise, the next turn in the path would reveal the tower of gray smoke from his burning cabin and the black circling buzzards. Out of any bush at any time might spring a warrior with upraised tomahawk. Every aspect of the frontiersman's life, from planting and harvesting to courting and raising a family, was directly affected by Indian hostility.

The border war was characterized by cunning, surprise, long marches, and sharp, bloody clashes. Its primary feature was the Indian raid, a tactic that had four definite stages: the approach, the attack, the gathering of loot, and the withdrawal.

Having decided upon some isolated cabin as their target, a group of a half dozen or so warriors would set out through the forest. At first the foray had the aspects of a holiday, the raiders traveling at a leisurely pace, stopping to hunt, bragging around the campfire about the brave deeds they would perform in battle. As they came closer to their objective, they began to move with greater care and speed. The last three days they fasted. On the third day—no matter how cold the weather—they stripped to moccasins and breechclout, having found that wounds healed better if bits of clothing weren't in them. Then they painted their face and body in grotesque designs of red, black, green, and yellow to terrify their victims.

They timed the approach to reach the target at dawn, always the favorite hour of attack.

The raiders lay in wait at the edge of the clearing until the men of the frontier family emerged in the gray light to do the morning chores. The signal for the assault was usually a birdcall. Shots crashed out. The eerie war whoop sounded, and the warriors charged with tomahawk and scalping knife.

If the attack was successful (and many were not, because of the leathery pluck of the frontiersmen), the Indians gathered together all the plunder the captured horses and prisoners could carry. Then, leaving the cabin in flames, they set off through the forest on a forced march to outdistance pursuit. Raiding parties were seldom overtaken.

The white captives were usually teen-age boys, who could be adopted into the tribe, and strong young women, who became slaves. The Southern red man badly mistreated his prisoners, but never raped the women. In his belief, this act would make him impure and therefore weaken him. After she had been adopted into the tribe and taught to practice its purification rites, one of these women might become the wife of a warrior. Adult white male captives were few and held in high esteem; they were taken back to the village to be tortured to death by the Indian women.

As suddenly as they came, however, the raids would subside. During one of these brief periods of peace, young Dale got his only formal education. He and his next oldest brother were sent to a boarding school about ten miles from the fort. But before long in the cold gray light of some forgotten dawn a slightly off-key birdcall triggered the sputter of musketry and the ringing war whoop. Shutters banged down on the cabin windows, and once more a state of siege settled upon the Southern frontier.

One morning Joe Horn and Dave Calhoun left Glade Hollow fort to plant corn in their clearings, foolishly taking their families with them. Afterward the two men left for a bit of hunting. They returned to find that the Shawnees had carried off both families intact. Horn and Calhoun rushed back to the fort almost insane with grief. Apparently neither of the wives nor any of the children were ever recovered.

A Glade Hollow woman named Ann Bush was captured with her infant son. As always, the Indians wanted to get away as quickly as possible; the young mother, encumbered by her child, was slowing them up. They killed and scalped the infant, then tomahawked and scalped Mrs. Bush, leaving her for dead.

Hours later she regained consciousness, bandaged her head with her apron, and staggered back to the fort with her dead son in her arms. As a boy Dale often heard her tell the story. Her face, loosened by the loss of her scalp, drooped in a tragic mask, and she always wore a bonnet.

Life at Glade Hollow was stark, mostly all work and precious little play. So when word came that Happy Kincaid and Sally McClure of nearby Clinch Mountain were about to be married, everyone in the fort was sorely tempted to go to the wedding. They knew the Shawnee were about, that they might be ambushed on the way, that on their return they might find the fort and all their belongings in ashes.

On the other hand, weddings on the Southern frontier were not an everyday event. Moreover, Sally McClure was a lovely, lively girl of seventeen, and her father was quite well-to-do. There would be a long table sagging with hams, turkeys, ducks, venison, pork roast, pies, cakes, roasting ears of corn, plenty of Monongahela whisky for the big folks, and enough dancing and laughter for all. Everyone in the fort decided to go, and off they went.

At Clinch Mountain they encountered a dreadful hush that was all too familiar. They found the McClure cabin a smoldering ruin, the long table an obscene feast set for the buzzards. Sprawled amid the smoky chaos were the scalped and mutilated corpses of McClure and a half dozen others. The raiders had slashed open pillows and mattresses for their cloth, dumping out the feathers, which fluttered about in a ghostly blizzard with each puff of wind.

Mrs. McClure, her infant son, an older boy, and two daughters—Sally and a younger sister named Peggy—had been carried off. Later that day Peggy came staggering back to what had been her home and gasped out the news to the wedding guests.

Her mother, carrying the baby, was holding the Indians up so they tore the child from her arms and killed him. As they were busy scalping him, Peggy saw a round sinkhole in the limestone formation at her feet and quietly stepped into it, falling about fifteen feet into a deep ravine, through which she made her escape.

Peggy was not the only one to escape, however. That night when the raiders stopped for a rest, they tied up the captives and went to sleep. Sally McClure, lying between two warriors, waited until they were snoring. Then she managed to loosen her deerhide thongs and slip away.

Pushing through the forest all night and the next day, she reached her homestead just before dark. Her fiancé and the guests had just finished burying the dead. Meanwhile, the preacher, a circuit rider, had arrived. At the graveside, with the acrid smoke from the cabin's embers drifting across the scene, and tears streaming down her cheeks, Sally McClure was married to Happy Kincaid. Later her mother and brother were recaptured.

Thus Sam Dale spent his boyhood—toughened to every hardship, living on the coarsest food, his weapons as much a part of him as his hands and feet, his life always in danger, constantly coming upon the gruesome remains of others who were not so plucky or lucky, putting his faith in God and loving the deep, dark, solemn forest to the end.

2

TRAPPED
IN
A
TREE

Toward the end of 1783 the Dales moved with the advancing frontier to the vicinity of what today is Greensboro, Georgia. They were then in the country of the Cherokee and the Creek.

The Indians promptly began their raids. The Dales and about thirty other families moved into Carmichael's Station, a fort with a palisade of sharpened logs and a blockhouse in one corner. Every day the men went out in squads, carrying a loaded rifle, the hammer up, to till the cornfields, tend the cattle, and hunt for game. They harvested several hundred bushels of corn, shucked it, and put the ears in a pen inside the palisade, leaving the husks piled in front.

One night Dale, then eleven years old, was awakened by sharp, yipping war whoops. He saw his father and mother, each wearing a sleeping cap and each holding a rifle, standing at the open door. They were silhouetted by a bright, flaring orange flame. The Indians had slipped into the fort and set fire to the corn husks.

"Sam," his father said, "take your brother and put that fire out."

Hardly awake, the two boys ran to the corn pen and, as Indian musket balls sang around them, tore off the rails. The ears tumbled down upon the husks, quickly smothering the fire. Leaving two dead, the Indians retreated. But everyone knew they were not far off.

One of the fort's best men, a Captain Autrey, went out on a scout. He didn't return. A search party found him, tomahawked, scalped, and mutilated.

One evening during this time young Dale accompanied his father and several other men on a ride though the purple forest to dig potatoes. The patch was surrounded by a rail fence. They let down the rails and rode into the patch, leaving the fence down to make escape easier if they were attacked.

They were just about to dismount in the ringing insect chorus of the Southern twilight, when someone yelled, "The fence is back up!"

"Every man for himself!" Dale's father roared.

There sounded a birdcall that was not quite the real thing. The party galloped for the fence. One by one each horse bunched, leaped, and raced for the forest, the rider hugging its neck, as all around powder flared in the pan and Indian muskets spat fire.

The bullets buzzed like bees, and the banging echoed in a steady thunder.

A musket ball stung the cartilage of young Dale's nose. But he and everyone else in the party returned to the fort, though several men were wounded and two horses were so badly hit they later had to be destroyed. For the rest of his life, Dale carried a small white scar on the tip of his nose.

"Every man for himself!" Those four words were the grim cry of the border. Frontier lore is filled with accounts of people forced to make agonizing decisions under Indian attack. There was the fleeing man who dropped his infant child in order to save its weakening mother. There was the man who strangled his dog to prevent its barking and giving away his family's hideout. There was the mother who slammed the cabin door in the faces of her children racing toward it in order to preserve those who had already reached safety.

The frontier people were superhumanly tough and accepted such decisions and their consequences as part of the feral life they had chosen to lead.

The children were no exception. Three days after the potato patch ambush, Dale and his next oldest brother slipped out from the fort to hunt coon. As a precaution, Dale had a flintlock pistol stuck in his belt. His brother was unarmed.

It was early morning. The grass was heavy with dew, and the beautifully intricate network of spider webs glistened in the first light of the sun as the two

boys walked through the clean, green-smelling forest
that was already loud with the calls of birds and the
frenzied arguments of squirrels.

On the edge of a glade they treed a coon, and Dale
climbed up to shake it loose. He was near the top of
the tree when he heard the loud, reverberating deto-
nations of gunfire close by. The brothers exchanged a
long look. Every boy for himself. The younger one ran
for the fort, and Dale gripped his tree while the forest
fell silent, as if holding its breath.

A Negro stumbled out of the underbrush, fell headlong into the glade, and lay still. A second Negro appeared, running floppily through the high grass, his
long blue tailcoat flying out behind him like a flag.
Then three Creek warriors appeared. Naked but for
moccasins and breechclout, their faces painted in a
hideous mask, arms and legs in garish rings, they
raced after the Negro, brandishing muskets and
tomahawks.

Dale watched in horror as the Negro ran straight
for his tree. The lead warrior, running easily, was
closing on his quarry. He reached out for the fluttering coattail, grabbed it. It tore off in his hands. He
grabbed the collar. The whole coat came off, and the
Indian fell, rolling head over heels in the wet grass.
With renewed strength, the Negro sprinted for the
fort. The Creek, war paint smeared, picked himself
up, tossed the coat away, and loped after him.

The other two warriors scalped the dead Negro,
taking the entire top of the head in the Creek fashion,
then sauntered across the sunny glade toward the

tree. Had they seen him? Dale cowered behind the trunk, trying to make his young body shrink. The two warriors walked to the tree and slowly raised their flat, black eyes. They had seen him. They stood, silently, gazing up at him with interest.

Dale looked down at them through the trembling leaves. They were standing close together. His pistol was loaded with buckshot. Maybe if he fired between them, he could get them both. There was only one chance, for he had no reload. He did have an advantage. The Indians were unaware that he was armed. Carefully hiding his actions behind the tree trunk, he reached down, pulled up the pistol from his belt, and hefted the long, weighty weapon in his fist.

The hammer was like the plumed head of a bird of prey, holding the piece of flint in its jaws. He checked the flint to be sure it wasn't worn and that it was firmly in place. Then he let go of the trunk. Balancing himself on his branch, he held the pistol in his right hand and pulled the hammer back with his left, then leaned forward to the trunk again.

The two painted faces were still close together as the Creeks quietly discussed how to take care of the white boy in the tree. He was about three stories up. The Indians were about forty feet away.

Quickly Dale swung the pistol around the right side of the trunk, leveled the heavy barrel, sighted down its length, and released the trigger. The hammer pecked forward, the flint struck sparks, and there was the hissing suck of the priming charge. Then the pistol bucked in his fist, shoving up his whole arm.

Crack a-whack a-whack a-whack. The shot echoed and re-echoed through the forest. Dale was blinded by the thick white sulphurous smoke that smelled like a rotten egg. Leisurely it drifted away in the morning breeze. Down through the bright, quivering leaves Dale saw that one of the Creeks was on his back and that he would never get up again. The other was running off. Dale gave a long, shuddering sigh of relief and started to climb up after the coon.

Then he stopped. The third Indian, the one with the smeared war paint, had given up his pursuit of the Negro and was coming across the sun-dappled forest floor. Carrying a musket, he walked up to Dale's tree. He looked down at his dead companion, then up at the boy who had killed him. The Creek's face was a black mask. He raised his musket.

"I have often been baffled for hours by a fox squirrel in a tree, watching my motions and going round and round, so as to keep the tree between me and him," Dale said later, recalling the incident. "I played the same game with the Indian."

The difference was that a squirrel is built for such work, with sharp claws on four feet. As Dale scrambled around the tree, he ripped his fingernails to the bloody quick, and the rough bark cut cruelly into his knees.

The Creek fired. Dale felt keen pain. In his mouth was the rusty taste of blood. But the ball hadn't hit him. It had thwacked into the tree close to his head, filling his face with flying bits of bark, some of which cut the skin. Anxiously the Indian peered up through

the drifting smoke cloud, grimacing when he saw the boy on his precarious perch, apparently unharmed.

Then Dale had a chance to catch his breath as the Creek went through the laborious process of reloading. But all too soon he shoved the ball down the barrel, and the game resumed.

The outcome was heavily weighted in favor of the red man. Putting a ball into his tiring, hurting target was only a matter of time. Presumably he knew, the way Indians knew things, that he had no reason to fear the boy's pistol. He ran back and forth, musket ready for the telling shot, as Dale kept up his jerky, painful circuit of the tree trunk. The boy knew that he could not keep up his dodging much longer.

The Creek fired, once more barking the tree inches from Dale's head. Stolidly, grimly, the Indian began to reload for the third shot, and Dale hauled air into his tortured lungs. He was almost done in. Even if the Creek didn't hit him the next time, he was about to fall out of the tree from exhaustion. The warrior rammed a ball home. Slowly he raised the musket. The boy watched as the single brown eye of the muzzle swung toward him.

There came the moan of bullets, then the popping of shots. Dale's father and a party from the fort were running toward the tree, firing as they ran. The Creek at once forgot the boy and raced across the bright glade into the forest. Dale climbed up, shook his coon loose, and with it on his belt walked back to the fort with his proud father.

*　　*　　*

In November, 1791, Dale Senior moved his family to a tract of land in the forest three miles southwest of Carmichael's Station, having agreed to pay for it with 7000 pounds of tobacco he planned to grow there.

The move was Mr. Dale's first business venture, but he was confident that it was the beginning of a new prosperous life for all of them. The whites and Indians were again living in peace. Everyone in the Dale family was happily looking forward to Christmas in the new home.

Then came the first reverse. The horses began to act strangely. They ran into things, stumbled in their gait, and frequently fell. They had the blind staggers. The disease killed all but one.

On Christmas Day Dale's mother died. Of what the frontiersman never divulged, but her illness was apparently brief. The blow was stunning to all of them, but the hardest hit was Dale's father. He hardly spoke or raised his head, wandering around the cabin like a ghost. Within a week he had joined his wife in the grave.

Shocked friends from Carmichael's Station came with small gifts of food, to commiserate with the children. On the harsh Southern frontier, where death by violence was so commonplace, for two members of the same family to die of natural causes within such a short time of each other was awesome indeed.

Dale was crushed, overpowered by the sense of being alone and helpless. At the age of nineteen, he was head of a family of eight brothers and sisters. They had no relatives to appeal to or friends who had enough to share with them. They were heavily in debt, living in a lonely cabin in a forest that teemed with Indians who might turn hostile at any moment.

The night after he buried his father, when his brothers and sisters had cried themselves to sleep, Dale slipped out to the tiny cemetery and prayed. "I went to the grave a brokenhearted, almost despairing boy," he said later. "I came back tearful and sad, but a hopeful and resolute man."

3

BIG
SAM

With hope and resolution, with grindingly hard work and self-denial, the Dales managed to hold out for two years. Fortunately nothing happened to make the Cherokees and Creeks turn hostile. The red men and the parentless family got along well together.

As he grew to full manhood, Dale became celebrated on the border for his prowess as a hunter and for great feats of strength. The Indians had the highest admiration for him, calling him Sam Thlucco, Big Sam.

Dale's biographer, J.F.H. Claiborne, who knew the frontiersman intimately, wrote:

General Dale was six feet two inches, erect, square-shouldered, rawboned and muscular, noted particularly for great length and strength of arm.

In many respects, physical and moral, he resembled his antagonists of the woods. He had the square forehead, the high cheekbones, the compressed lips—in fact the physiognomy of the Indian, relieved, however, by a fine benevolent Saxon eye.

Like the Red Man, too, his foot fell lightly upon the ground. He spoke slowly and in low tones, and seldom laughed. I observed of him what has been often noticed as peculiar to border men of high attributes—he entertained a strong attachment for the Indians, extolled their courage, their tenderness to their children, and their reverence for the dead.

I have often seen a wretched remnant of the Choctaws, homeless and oppressed, camped around his plantation, and subsisting on his bounty. In peace, even the Creeks entertained for him the highest veneration. He fed many when gaunt famine, more terrible even than the "dogs of war," pursued them; but in battle the name of Big Sam fell on the ear of the (Creek) like that of Marius on the hordes of the Cimbri.

Claiborne considered Dale an excellent example of what he called the genuine frontiersman:

... modest, truthful, patient, frugal, full of religious faith, proud of his country—remorseless in battle, yet prompt to forgive, and ever ready to jeopard his own safety for the helpless and oppressed—a race

of men such as no other country had produced—
wholly American—a feature as prominent in our
social and political history as the grand physical
characteristics peculiar to this continent.

Other, more recent writers have found the frontiersmen rather lacking in such sterling qualities, describing them as crude, loudmouthed ruffians who,
when no red men were available, joyfully leaped
upon their fellow whites. Claiborne perhaps would
argue that they were not the genuine frontiersman. In
any case, among the border people there were such
truly outstanding men as Daniel Boone, John Robert-
son, James Sevier, and Sam Dale.

The Indians frequently visited the Dale farm, trading game and pelts for tobacco, a weed that had great
religious significance to them over and above the
pleasure they received in smoking it. But more and
more white men began to push into the area, and the
migration touched off renewed warfare.

In 1793, when Dale was twenty-one, the governor
of Georgia authorized a Captain Foote to organize a
troop of horse to protect the frontier. Dale got an old
man to run the farm in his absence and volunteered
for the duty. Wearing a coonskin cap, bearskin vest,
and homespun hunting shirt, with a wallet of parched
corn and a blanket tied behind their saddle, and carrying a long rifle and a hunting knife, the scouts rode
out on extended tours of the border.

Within a few months they were mustered into the
United States Army and ordered to Fort Mathews on

the Oconee River, Georgia. Dale's salary and an excellent crop of tobacco permitted him to pay off more than half the price of the land and to lay in a heavy supply of provisions. The following year he was able to discharge the debt in full.

But the same year the Creeks suddenly rose up, killing, burning, driving off livestock. Dale's company pursued a raiding party on foot to its village on the west bank of the Chattahoochee River, deep in hostile territory. The scouts reached the east bank at dark and settled down to wait for the dawn.

It was a long time coming. The black river slid unhurriedly past, glittering with starshine. The night was filled with the aggravating song of thirsty mosquitoes, the sigh and rattle of the canebrake, and the croaking, burping, belching of the frogs among the lily pads.

Slowly, imperceptibly, the dark blue faded from the sky, and the river became a muddy brown. In the dead gray light the scouts stepped into the cold, pushing water and, holding their rifle and powder horn high, waded across the river toward the long roll of cottony mist that lay along the opposite bank under the dark trees. Like dripping phantoms, they slipped into the village and took up a position in the square, facing the wooden, thatch-roofed cabins. A sleepy-eyed Indian stumbled out of a doorway; his eyes snapped open, he yelled, and died.

Half-naked Creeks charged out of the cabins with whatever weapon came to hand. The rifle fire cut down many. Many more kept coming. No time to reload. Dale and the others clubbed their weapon and fought the red man hand to hand in the thick smelly gunsmoke that filled the square.

The battle lasted only minutes. The scouts killed thirteen Creeks and captured ten for hostages. The others escaped into the woods. Then the white men set fire to the village, and as the bright, roaring red flames ate up the cabins the scouts led their tightly bound captives back across the river.

To avoid ambush they took a different route home. Dale was reconnoitering ahead. In a canebrake he came upon a cabin. Two Creeks rushed out, each leveling a musket. Dale raised his rifle and shot one warrior dead. The other leaped into the cane. As Dale finished reloading, another scout, a man named O'Neal, ran up. Together he and Dale began to worm their way through the dense, rattling cane after the second Indian.

A shot exploded not twenty yards off, and O'Neal fell dead. The rest of the company came charging up then and opened a steady fire into the cane. Bullets clipped the stalks all around Dale. He lay back in the muck, drawing O'Neal's corpse over him as a shield. Ball after ball thumped into the Irishman's body. Two wounded Dale slightly. Still the fusillade kept up.

"It was some time," the frontiersman reported dryly, "before the fire slackened sufficiently for me to apprise them of my position."

Once apprised, the scouts promptly began to shoot into the other side of the thicket. Dale struggled out from under the dead weight of the protecting corpse and lay gasping for breath. Then he heard a rattle and saw the second Creek crawling toward him on his belly like a snake, knife in hand. Dale sat up, cocked his rifle lock, sighted on the Indian's weaving forehead, and squeezed the trigger.

There was a flare and a small puff of smoke—a flash in the pan. The vent was clogged with mud.

Before Dale could reprime, before he could club his rifle, before he could even change his awkward position, the warrior was upon him, his left hand twisted in Dale's long hair, the knife at his throat, the momentum of his hurtling body throwing Dale on his back. The frontiersman grabbed at the knife hand, but the point closed upon his throat; above the blade the two enemies stared into each other's widened eyes, just inches apart.

A shot. With the strength of desperation, Dale managed to throw over the Creek. He scrambled to his feet, snatching his own knife from its sheath, and plunged the blade into the warrior's chest. But he was stabbing a dead man. The shot, fired by a scout named Murray, had found the Indian's heart.

"He was a brave fellow," Dale said. "So we wrapped his blanket around him, broke his gun and laid it across his body, and departed."

Soon afterward Dale was assigned ten men and picketed at Fort Republic on the Appalachee River. The duty was exhausting and full of peril. Five days out of every six, either singly or in pairs, the scouts reconnoitered the border, making a circuit of twenty-five miles a day.

Typically Dale traveled alone. On one reconnaissance he rode until twilight settled over the forest. He stopped at a stream, watered his horse, then tethered it at a clump of bushes near a gnarled oak. He made a paste of the parched corn and ate it with his knife, washing it down with a long drink from the stream. The bats were out, zipping around like frantic winged mice in the darkling sky. The moon came up, a full moon, bright orange, warm-looking, and awesomely huge when it first appeared through the black trunks of the trees. Then, as it climbed from branch to black branch, it grew smaller, paler, colder-looking, and more remote.

Watching the moon, Dale contentedly smoked a pipe. At last he wrapped himself in his blanket and lay down between the big, wall-like roots of the oak. Lulled by the whispering roar of the wind and breathing deeply of the forest air, he was soon asleep.

Frontiersmen, those who survived, were not heavy sleepers. Particularly when they were in the field, they slept lightly, as if "with one eye open." Dale was awakened by the nervous snorting of his horse. He sat up, instantly alert, and tore the blanket off him.

Almost at once a pack of wolves came bounding toward him through the trees, barking and snarling, eyes like coals in the moonlight. Dale scurried up the oak like a squirrel. A wolf leaped after his scrambling feet and locked its teeth on one of the boots. The snarling weight hung there a long moment, the other wolves waiting expectantly. The boot slipped off; the wolf fell back; Dale bolted up the tree.

He sat on a high branch, embracing the trunk, as the wolves madly circled and recircled the tree, snarling at him, leaping up, clawing the ground, gnawing the oak as if trying to cut it down with their teeth. Strangely enough they never bothered the horse, which nonetheless spent the night screaming in terror, fortunately rousing Dale each time he dozed.

At last dawn brought the frontiersman's uncomfortable vigil to an end. The wolves stalked off, having first ripped the blanket and boot to shreds.

The history of the border was the constant breaking out of still another Indian war. Even when trouble had been brewing for some time, the first mad assault always came as a surprise—almost as much of one to the red men as to the white men. The forests were blood-soaked before there was real peace.

During this period of his career, Dale was often sent on long scouts into the Creek Nation to spy upon the villages and eavesdrop on their councils in an attempt to give some warning if another attack was planned. On these scouts, to avoid detection, he never built a fire, subsisting entirely on his wallet of parched corn, and he always went afoot.

Returning from a mission one hot summer afternoon, still deep in Creek country and dizzy with thirst, he bent over a mountain brook to drink. The water came tumbling higgledy-piggledy, roaring and flashing, down through the mossy rocks and great twisted roots. Dale could hear nothing but its pleasant noise. He had hardly noticed the big log behind him.

He was just about to put his lips to the stream when he caught the dark reflection of two warriors looming up from behind the log, tomahawks flashing in the sun. Snapping his arms straight, Dale lifted up his torso as in a push-up and gathered his legs under him. The first brave came charging forward. Dale took his tomahawk hand and, with a quick heave, pitched him over his shoulder into the brook.

The frontiersman, whirled, crouching, to face the second Creek with knife extended. Dodging the first wild slash of the tomahawk, he tangled with the brave and ran him through.

The first Indian clambered out of the water and into Dale's arms. Grunting, gasping, slipping on the moss-slick rocks, trying to twist a leg behind the other's knee to throw him down, red man and white grappled on the edge of the merry mountain brook, red man with tomahawk, white man with knife, hacking, parrying, jabbing. The red man was strong, the white man stronger. The Creek sighed his life out and fell away from the scarlet blade.

Then finally Dale had his drink. Clean, cold, sweet, wet—nothing had ever tasted better. At last he realized that he had received five separate tomahawk slashes in the fight, though he had no recollection of getting even one. But characteristically, he did not stop to lick his wounds.

He had met two Indians and bested them in combat. Most men, even frontiersmen, would have been satisfied. Such an encounter was enough to make one a minor hero on the Southern—or any other—border.

Sam Dale, however, was not a minor hero. Of all the qualities that summed him up, the paramount one was his incredible combativeness. When there was fighting in the air, Dale was the last to sheath his knife, even when his opponents were the most pugnacious Indians, for whom hand-to-hand combat was a way of life and an art they had practiced since boyhood.

Figuring that two Creeks meant more Creeks, Dale decided to retrace the warriors' trail to their camp. He set out at once through the long green Southern forest afternoon, moving steadily to keep his wounds from stiffening. He followed the somewhat pigeon-toed tracks of the two dead men across the bare ground. In the bright, sweaty glades he noted the telltale streak of bent grass that marked their passage. In the cool depths of the forest he observed the trail of bent twigs, the moss brushed off the tree trunks, and the dark underside of leaves flipped over by the Creeks' passing feet.

Nine grueling miles he traced the trail through the forest. Several times he lost it, but soon picked it up again. Despite his efforts, his wounds had begun to stiffen. The afternoon grew cooler. The westering sun sent shafts of golden light slanting down through the trees, and the shadows were pushing out long and dark on the forest floor when an exciting smell came to Dale's nostrils—woodsmoke.

Following his nose, he crawled to the campsite. He peered around the side of a boulder. Three Creek braves were snoring by the fire, wrapped in the shroud of their blankets. Lying between two of them, tightly bound, her dress in shreds, flesh cut by brambles, was a young white woman. She was awake, staring dully into the flames as if seeing her wretched future.

Dale stepped out from behind the rock. Signaling to the woman for silence, he slipped from one Indian to the next and eased the knife into each chest. He had just finished cutting the woman's leather thongs when a fourth Creek, a huge warrior, leaped out from behind a tree, knife upraised, screaming. He hurled himself upon the frontiersman, who went down heavily.

Weak from his wounds and the long trek, Dale had no fight left in him. Though he had two hands on the Creek's knife hand, the blade came down steadily, and Dale got ready to die. The Indian pressed on.

There was a thunk, a grunt, and the Creek's body landed on Dale like a felled oak. The woman had snatched up a tomahawk and sunk it into the Indian's head. Dale wrapped the woman in the least bloody of the blankets and escorted her to the nearest fort.

In a romantic story the frontiersman and the young woman would have fallen in love and been married. They did, after all, owe a great deal to each other, and they had shared an intensely dramatic experience. Apparently, however, he never saw her again.

Dale had the fullest appreciation and admiration for women, both white and red, but he never married. He was a sensitive man in a world that had no place for sensitivity, a world in which death by violence was commonplace. Perhaps he had seen too many families massacred or at least broken up in the Indian wars to want to take the chance that a family of his would survive intact.

Certainly he realized that, with the perilous life he had picked for himself, the odds were all against his surviving any length of time. And on the rigorous frontier, as he had seen in his own case, a family without a father was in a desperate situation.

Whatever his reason, Big Sam Dale went through life as he stalked the forest—alone.

4

THE
DEATH
OF
DOUBLEHEAD

For a while the Southern Indians lost interest in their "beloved occupation." In 1796, as peace settled along the Southern border, Dale's outfit was disbanded.

That winter the frontiersman bought a four-horse wagon and went to Savannah to haul freight. With spring, he returned to the tobacco farm to help his brothers and sisters with the crop. Later he began to trade with the Creeks, bartering his calico, gunpowder, whisky, and gewgaws for their hides and pelts.

Men got rich in this business, but not Sam Dale. The money came easily; it went much more easily. To Dale a man's word was his bond, a firm handshake more important than a signature (or mark) on the dotted line. He was openhearted, openhanded, to the point of foolishness. And yet the forest was so big, so utterly full of nature's bounty, that it seemed a cornucopia that could never be exhausted.

In 1799, another great wave of white men surged into the Mississippi Territory, the present states of Mississippi and Alabama. Dale bought three wagons and teams, and he transported scores of families to the new frontier.

Then, in 1803, President Thomas Jefferson, a far-sighted Easterner who could see that the future of the United States lay in the West, ordered a highway to be marked out through the wilderness to the Mississippi Territory. Dale and a half blood named Elick Saunders were selected as guides. When he had finished blazing the trail, Dale set up a trading post among the Cherokees in Tennessee.

In 1807, having received word of a big Indian ball game on the Hiwassee River in the southeastern part of the state, Dale took a line of packhorses loaded with goods to the site of the contest. As usual, the ball game was taking place in the fall of the year, the time of the harvest. More than a thousand red men were assembled on the river, along with a number of white traders and some United States Army officers from Hiwassee Fort.

Before the game began, Dale plied his trade, then strolled up to Doublehead, the great chief of the Cherokees. A tall, stalwart man with an ugly, pock-marked face, Doublehead was one of the most feared Indians on the entire American frontier. He had hated white men ever since they had treacherously killed his brother, Old Tassel, in 1788. Since then Doublehead had avenged the death many, many times over. He was a powerful orator, and in personal combat he had never met his match. His sudden furies were dreaded even by his own people.

Doublehead was on the edge of the playing field, with a few other Indians and whites, standing by a huge pile of blankets, trinkets, saddles, and other items that the two opposing towns had bet on the contest. Nearby, players were getting tattooed before the game.

Seeing Dale, Doublehead scowled. "Big Sam," he growled, "you are a mighty liar."

Bristling, Dale demanded, "What do you mean embarrassing me like this in front of these people?"

Doublehead grinned. "You have never kept your promise to come and see me."

He hated white men but he liked Dale. And Dale liked—or at least respected—him. He did not hold Doublehead's bloody past against him. It was the violent way of the frontier. As they waited for the game to begin, Doublehead broke out a bottle of Monongahela.

On the border just about everyone drank. The white man who became a drunk, however, usually got that way only after many years of hard work at it. The red man, on the other hand, fell victim to alcoholism almost as readily as he did to smallpox and the other diseases Europeans had brought with them from across the great lake. But the Indian loved hard liquor, and when there was any around he could seldom be kept from it.

The little party passed Doublehead's bottle around, swigging the strong, oily tasting rye whisky. They soon finished the bottle. Dale had a few bottles in his packtrain and offered to get one, but Doublehead shook his ugly head. "When I am in the white man's country, I drink his liquor," he rumbled. "But here you must drink Doublehead's."

He produced another bottle as the opposing teams, which represented most of the young men and women from the two towns, took their places on the field. One team was painted white. Each player carried a racket with a handle about three feet long and a netting of rawhide. The hard little deerskin ball was tossed up in the center of the field. With a wild cheer and the clash of rackets, the game was on.

Indians called their ball "the little brother of war," an apt description. The game has come down to the present time as lacrosse, still a very rugged sport. But, as the Indians played ball, it was the closest thing possible to warfare without the lifting of scalps and the burning of the other side's players. Black eyes and bloody noses were common, and the girls on the team were not spared. A great ballplayer was respected almost as highly as a great warrior.

As Doublehead's party was watching the game, a Cherokee captain named Bone-polisher came up to the chief and denounced him as a traitor for having sold a piece of the tribe's land to white speculators. Doublehead remained silent, which only increased Bone-polisher's anger. Steadily he became louder and more abusive. The chief took the outburst, eyes downcast, though Dale could see the rage swelling up inside him.

At last Doublehead drew a deep breath and fixed his glittering eyes upon his assailant. "Go away," he growled. "You have said enough. Leave me or I'll kill you."

With a scream of rage, Bone-polisher charged, swinging a tomahawk. Doublehead took the blow full on his left forearm, jerking a pistol from his belt with the other hand. There was a loud report, a cloud of smoke, and Bone-polisher lay on his back, dead in the dirt.

Drawn by the shot, the crowd and the sweaty ball-players, carrying their battered rackets, ran up to see what was wrong. Fighter though he was, Dale was worried. This fight was not his. Having seen that Doublehead's wound was taken care of, he rode off with his packtrain for the Hiwassee ferry.

In a cabin on the bank of the slow, tawny river, he found his old friend and fellow guide Elick Saunders, along with a Cherokee chieftain named Ridge and John Rogers, an elderly full-blooded white man who had lived much of his life among the Cherokees.

As always, just before twilight, the birds and animals fell silent and a great green hush settled upon the forest. Twilight came and then, quickly, the misty autumn night. The men in the cabin lighted a candle in the iron lantern on the table, and the slivers of yellow light flickered across the faces and the walls as they sat drinking mugs of coffee, quietly discussing the fight.

The conversation was guarded on both sides. What Doublehead had done was nothing new. Many chiefs —usually under the influence of the white man's liquor—had sold pieces of land to speculators, keeping the money for themselves. Though the Indians were angry, they usually did nothing out of respect for their leader. Doublehead was well thought of by his people, at least most of them. Dale did not know how the others at the table felt about the chief and he didn't want to find out, although he had his suspicions.

Some time after nightfall there was a pounding at the door. It was opened and Doublehead, his arm in a bloody bandage, came in, followed by several companions. Dale was less than glad to see them. He was strictly neutral and had no desire to get involved in an intestine feud. If he did, he might well be the cause of a war between his people and the Indians.

Doublehead seemed to appreciate the frontiersman's awkward position and tried to keep peace in the stuffy little cabin. Rogers, however, soon began to lash out at the chief, upbraiding him just as Bonepolisher had done earlier. With singular forbearance for a man of his explosive nature, Doublehead made no reply. The white man began to scream at him. Finally Doublehead held up his bloody arm. "I have let you live among us," he rumbled. "But I have never seen you in any of our councils or on the warpath with us. You have no place among the chiefs of our people. Be silent and interfere with me no more."

The old man continued to scream at him. For the

second time that day, and with an air of resignation, Doublehead drew his pistol; he leveled it between the white man's startled eyes and pulled the trigger. The hammer snapped, sparks flew, but the pistol did not fire. Doublehead had forgotten to reload after killing Bone-polisher.

Ridge reached out a long arm and swept the lantern off the table. In the sudden dark there came the flash and slow roar of another pistol, the crash of the door being thrown open, and the thud of running feet. Dale fumbled about in the smoke-choked blackness until he found the lantern and relighted it. Doublehead lay prone on the puncheon floor, blood oozing steadily from his ruined lower jaw.

Dale helped the chief's companions bandage the wound. Then the Indians started to carry Doublehead through the forest to Hiwassee Fort. Worried about being overtaken by their enemies, however, they left him in the barn of a schoolmaster named Black. Warriors from Bone-polisher's clan followed the spotted trail of blood and killed the Cherokee chief in the barn.

So ended the mighty Doublehead. Dale felt bad about the murder and his helplessness to avert it. He held no blame for the Indians involved.

"The cupidity of the speculators, who have so often robbed and ruined the Red Men, tempted Doublehead to sell a portion of his country," the frontiersman said. "From that moment his death was resolved upon. The rencounter with the Bone-polisher, where he acted strictly in self-defense, merely precipitated his fate. He perished apparently upon the Indian maxim of blood for blood, but was really the victim of conspiracy."

5

TECUMSEH
TALKS
WAR

For the next several years Dale continued to trade
with the Indians and to guide white settlers into the
Mississippi Territory. In 1811 a group of thirty Creek
chiefs assembled in Washington City, as the capital of
the United States was then known, and agreed to
permit the Americans to cut a horse path through the
Indian nation from the Chattahoochee River to the
Alabama River.

The "horse path," which the white people called
the Federal Road, became a highway that soon was
filled with wagonloads of settlers. Watching the relentless march into their homeland, the Indians grew
increasingly disturbed.

In October of 1811 the Creeks gathered at Took-a-
batcha, an ancient town on the Tallapoosa River, in
their annual grand council. Also on hand were Colo-

nel Benjamin Hawkins, the United States agent to the Creek nation, and his good friend, Sam Dale.

Since the death of the half-blooded chief, Alexander McGillivray, in 1793, Colonel Hawkins had assumed the major responsibility for leading the Indians. A kind and competent person, he had taught them to till the soil and collect livestock. The Creeks had thus begun the difficult transition from a primitive to a civilized culture that no other red men had been able to achieve. Many braves, however, bitterly resented the change.

The Creeks, whose lush homeland covered most of the present states of Georgia and Alabama, as well as part of Mississippi, were the most powerful of all Indian nations east of the Mississippi River. They numbered about 20,000 of whom more than 5000 were warriors, or gunmen, as contemporary white accounts called them.

Contrary to the stereotype of the glum, grunting red men, the Creeks were talkative and gay. Their language was pleasing to the ear—gentle, courteous, and musical, with no *r* sounds and not gutteral. The conversation of the women was said to resemble the twittering of birds.

The men were tall, erect, robust. Many were more than six feet—a great height in those days. Their skin was dark copper, and they decorated it with tattoos of flowers, animals, and the sun, moon, and stars. The greater the warrior, the more the tattoos. They shaved their head, leaving only a crest at the crown for a scalplock. The women were small, seldom taller than five feet, but well-formed, with big, round, black eyes. They were very affectionate and made excellent mothers.

For nearly three hundred years, since Pánfilo de Narváez's Spanish conquistadors first appeared on their frontier in 1528, the Creeks had been successfully fighting off the white intruders. As violently as they had resisted their military invasions, however, they welcomed them socially. For generations, Creek girls had married white traders. Consequently, many of the nation's warriors and chiefs were of mixed blood—and some of them were more white man than red.

Nevertheless, there was little evidence of white influence as the council gathered. The old town had an air of anticipation. A rumor had circulated throughout the nation and beyond that some Indians from the northwest, the Great Lakes country, would be present. On horseback and afoot, some 5000 red men came trooping through the forest to Took-a-batcha. Besides the Creeks were a number of Cherokees and Choctaws, many of whom had traveled for weeks to attend the meeting.

The rumor proved to be well-founded. The day after the council met the mighty Shawnee chief Tecumseh marched into the square, followed by twenty-four of his braves. They wore fringed buckskin shirts and leggings, fitted tightly to show their powerful muscular development. Dale had never seen a more athletic body of men. Each carried a rifle and a war club—a weapon new to this part of the country.

Their long black hair hung in three plaits, the temple closely shaved. Each wore a silver band around his forehead, with plumes of hawk and eagle feathers in his hair. Tecumseh himself wore two long crane feathers—one white, a symbol of peace and the other red, a symbol of war. A small red dot was painted on each temple. Semicircles of red were under each eye, and a large red dot was on the chest.

At forty-three, Tecumseh was in the prime of his quick, violent life. Since the Revolutionary War he had been the most consistently hostile of all Indian chiefs. He had studied with the great Shawnee, Cornstalk, whom white men had murdered while on a peace mission. His father and two of his brothers also had been killed in battles with the white man. A third brother, Seekaboo, a reformed drunk, was considered a holy man by the Indians, who called him The Prophet; he was in the Shawnee chief's party too. Though he hated his enemies as only an Indian could, Tecumseh had won a reputation among them for mercy and his opposition to the torture of prisoners. Tall, lean, straight, with a light copper skin, he was a magnificent figure of a man.

As they entered the square, Tecumseh and his braves gave no sign of recognition of anyone or anything, looking to neither right nor left. They marched to the big red council house and halted before it, standing like wooden Indians, as 5000 red men watched tensely.

A long pause. Then Menewa, Big Warrior, the enormous Creek chief who ruled at Took-a-batcha, went forward with the calumet—a pipe with a stem full four feet long, sheathed in a speckled snakeskin and hung with strings of wampum. Silently, he handed it to Tecumseh, who silently accepted it, took a puff and blew the thick gray smoke out first to the sky—to the Great Spirit—and then to the north, east, south, and west. One by one, his braves repeated his action. After this ceremony, Big Warrior pointed to the large log cabin that was to be the Shawnees' quarters while the guests of the Creeks. Tecumseh and his escort solemnly marched to it. Not a word had been uttered.

That night the Shawnees did the Dance of the Lakes, an eerie performance in which they made every muscle of their body quiver and shake as if in an epileptic seizure. Curious, the Southern Indians crowded around to watch the strange dance. Still nobody spoke.

The next few days the Indians spent purifying themselves for the conference by taking "the black drink," a powerful tea brewed from holly leaves that made them explosively sick to their stomach. The air was filled with the smoke of their pipes and the fluttering beat of the little deer-hide finger drums.

Each morning Tecumseh sent a messenger to the council house with the report that he would speak that day. But the long day dragged on and no Tecumseh. Then another messenger came with the same report: "The sun has traveled too far. Tecumseh will speak tomorrow."

After several days of this performance, Colonel

Hawkins lost patience and ordered his horses packed.

Dale took him aside. "The Shawnees mean mischief," he said. "You would do well to stay."

Hawkins pooh-poohed the idea. "The Creeks are entirely under my control," he told the frontiersman. "Tecumseh's visit is just for ceremony and show." He added with a gay laugh, "Sam, you're getting womanly and cowardly."

"There's danger ahead," Dale muttered. But he packed up and rode off with the Creek agent. At Big Spring, twelve miles away, they pitched camp. Then, having received Hawkins's condescending promise to wait for him there, Dale slipped back through the forest, alone and afoot.

On the path he ran into Bill Milfort, a half blood he had once nursed through a serious illness. Strongly attached to Dale, Milfort agreed to notify him when Tecumseh would speak. Then Dale hid out in a leafy bower as his friend went back to Took-a-batcha.

The sun was directly overhead next day when Milfort returned. "Tecumseh speaks tonight," he said.

With darkness, Dale stole through the sleeping forest. Took-a-batcha stood out in the black woods like a city of light. Council fires sent great spirals of sparks swirling up into the still autumn night and threw a flashing orange glare on the flat surface of the river.

Dale crept from lodge to dark lodge until he had a good view of the fiery square. He waited, along with 5000 Indians who stood densely packed together, all eyes upon the Shawnee cabin.

Slowly the door opened. Tecumseh stepped out,

followed in single file by his escort. Despite the cold-
ness of the night, the men were naked but for a loin
flap and moccasins. They were painted black from
head to toe—the primary color of war. Each carried a
war club. All were scowling.

"They looked," Dale told his biographer, "like a
procession of devils."

His face like a fist, Tecumseh marched stiffly
around the square, the other Shawnees coming after
in his steps. At each corner he stopped, took a pinch
of tobacco from the pouch by his loin flap, and
dropped it on the ground, his men doing the same.

Three times they marched around the square,
dropping pinches of tobacco. Then they strode to the
center and, facing north, emptied all the pouches on
the fire burning at the base of the tall pole there. At
last they drew up before the council house, in front of
which Big Warrior and his captains sat cross-legged,
watching intently. As before, not a word had been
spoken.

Tecumseh gave the shrill war whoop of the Shawnee, and the forest gloom echoed with a shocking
howl as his men answered. Striding forward stiffly,
Tecumseh took a wampum belt from his loin flap and
presented it to Big Warrior. It went from hand to
hand down the line of seated Creek captains.

The calumet came out and was smoked with the
same grave ceremony as before. In the tense quiet the
only sound was the secretive rustle of falling leaves. A
chilly dampness came over Took-a-batcha as the
autumn mist settled upon the forest. Five thousand

red men and a white man held their breath, waiting.

Then Tecumseh began to speak. He spoke slowly at first and in sonorous tones. But soon he worked himself up, and the words gushed from his lips. His eyes flared in the firelight, and his naked, painted body trembled with emotion. Now his voice sank to a low, musical key, now it rose to its highest, screaming pitch. At times his black face twisted with a sneer of hatred, at other times his teeth flashed in a murderous smile.

"I have heard many great orators," Dale said. "But I never saw one with the verbal powers of Tecumseh, or the same command of the muscles of his face. Had I been deaf, the play of his countenance would have told me what he said."

The Shawnee's words burned themselves into the frontiersman's mind:

In defiance of the white warriors of Ohio and Kentucky, I have traveled through their settlements—once our favorite hunting grounds. No war whoop was sounded, but there is blood on our knives. The palefaces felt the blow, but knew not whence it came.

Accursed be the race that has seized on our country and made women of our warriors. Our fathers, from their tombs, reproach us as slaves and cowards. I hear them now in the wailing winds. The Creek was once a mighty people. The Georgian trembled at your war whoop, and the maidens of my tribe on the distant lakes sang the prowess of your warriors and sighed for their embraces.

Now your very blood is white. Your tomahawks have no edge. Your bows and arrows are buried with your fathers. Oh, Creeks! Brush from your eyelids the sleep of slavery. Once more strike for vengeance—once more for your country. The spirits of the mighty dead complain. Their tears drop from the weeping skies.

Tecumseh brandished his war club.

Let the white race perish! They seize your land, they corrupt your women, they trample on the ashes of your dead! Back, whence they came upon a trail of blood, they must be driven. Back, back, aye, into the great water whose accursed waves brought them to our shores!

Burn their dwellings! Destroy their stock! Slay their wives and children! The red man owns the country, and the palefaces must never enjoy it! War now! War forever! War upon the living! War upon the dead! Dig their very corpses from the grave! Our country must give no rest to a white man's bones!

Thousands of tomahawks flashed in the firelight as the Shawnee's audience roared approval. Tecumseh's speech pleased the crowd, for nothing was closer to the Southern Indian's heart than war.

Even Big Warrior was moved. He had always been a good friend of the white man, but more than once Dale saw his huge paw convulsively clutch the handle of his knife. Perhaps he was remembering when he was known as Hothlepoya, the Crazy War Hunter, whose exploits in raids upon Indian tribes across the Tennessee had woven around his gigantic frame a tradition like that of Robin Hood and Rob Roy in the old country.

Tecumseh went on:

This is the will of the Great Spirit, revealed to my brother, his familiar, the Prophet of the Lakes. All the tribes of the North are dancing the war dance. Two mighty warriors across the seas will send us arms. Tecumseh will soon return to his country. My prophets shall tarry with you. They will stand between you and the bullets of your enemies. When the white men approach you, the yawning earth shall swallow them up.

Soon shall you see my arm of fire stretched athwart the sky. I will stamp my foot at Tippecanoe, and the very earth shall shake!

Tecumseh had spoken. The hush was electric. The Shawnee and his escort took their place by the seated Creeks. The long pipe passed puff by puff down the line.

Then, with no warning, the Shawnees leaped up and sounded their war cry. The night was ghastly with the responding whoops of their audience. Flourishing their war clubs and screaming, the Shawnees performed their tribal war dance, acting out the parts of a battle—scout, ambush, combat—as Dale slipped away.

At Big Spring he roused the sleeping Hawkins and gave his report. The white-haired agent heard Dale through, but still seemed oblivious to the great danger that threatened the entire frontier. Fully confident of his hold upon the Indians, Colonel Hawkins believed that any trouble that might arise would be only among the Creeks themselves and that he would be able to keep the fighting localized.

"He was an old and faithful officer," Dale said, "a man of fine sense, a sterling patriot, and of cool and unflinching courage. He loved the Indians; they had great confidence in him; but he was, unhappily, deceived on this occasion."

Arguing heatedly, the two men rode through the long, dark forest night.

Dale kept thinking of the Shawnee's speech. There were a couple of things in it that puzzled him mightily. The two warriors from across the sea were, of course, England and Spain. But what was Tecumseh's arm of fire? And what did he mean when he said he would stamp his foot at Tippecanoe and the ground would shake?

6

TECUMSEH'S
ARM
OF
FIRE

Tecumseh had come to the South on his speaking tour, because every sign pointed to the conclusion that the United States and Great Britain were going to war again—and soon. That the two nations were in such a confrontation was due to a number of factors, chief among which was the inexorable aggressiveness of the American frontiersman.

He had his own foreign policy, which had nothing to do with the foreign policy of his national government (a far-distant legislative body that he did not take at all seriously). The men of the border wanted land, land, evermore land in this teeming, wonderful, seemingly endless forest country. To get the land, they were prepared to use whatever force was necessary.

Blocking them were three powerful foes: the British, the Spanish, and the Indians. The frontiersmen, with their supreme self-confidence, were perfectly willing to take them all on. Apparently, by the end of 1811, they would have to do just that—and at the same time.

Bitter enemies for centuries, England and Spain had become secret allies in the topsy-turvy state of Old World geopolitics. Their mutual enemy was France, which England had been fighting almost steadily since 1793. Both the English and the Spanish had a big stake in America, which they were anxious to protect.

The British, in violation of the Treaty of Paris, which had ended the American Revolutionary War, still held onto their forts along the Great Lakes. Though Napoleon Bonaparte had forced Spain to give back to France the huge colony of Louisiana, which he then sold to the United States, the Spaniards were still firmly ensconced in Florida. They also claimed a strip along the lower part of the present states of Alabama and Mississippi, as well as the entire southwestern part of the North American continent.

The British refused to accept the validity of the transfer of Louisiana to the Americans. Both the British and Spanish were deeply concerned about the growing strength of the United States. Determined to prevent this strength from increasing, they were only too glad to supply the Indians with arms and ammunition to assault the American frontier.

The British munitions flowed out of Fort Malden,

England's western headquarters at the mouth of the Detroit River. Spain supplied the Indians from her base at Pensacola.

But the principal danger was the British naval blockade of Napoleonic Europe, which had caused a serious depression on the Western and Southern borders. The frontiersmen began to clamor for war against Great Britain. In Congress their fiery young representatives, who were called War Hawks and included Henry Clay of Kentucky and John C. Calhoun of South Carolina, were daily making speeches demanding war.

Tecumseh, the most brilliant Indian strategist since Pontiac, knew that the international situation presented a golden opportunity to the red man. With England and Spain for allies—and France far too busy in Europe to aid the United States as she had in the Revolutionary War—the Indians might be able to drive the Americans out of the country. First, however, the tribes would have to unite and wage war as a single army. Since the beginning of the trouble between the two races, this failure of the Indians to fight together had been the cause of all their major defeats at the hands of the white man.

Tecumseh's speech at Took-a-batcha was one of many he made in the Southeast in 1811, trying to get the Choctaws, Chickasaws, Cherokees, and Creeks to join with the Northern tribes in a confederation stretching from the Great Lakes to the Gulf of Mexico and dedicated to the single mission of pushing the

Americans, as he said, "back into the great water whose accursed waves brought them to our shore."

The Southern Indians were always ready to indulge in their beloved occupation. But the frontiersmen had beaten them before and might well again. They were wary of taking up the tomahawk against the tough Americans at this time. What Tecumseh needed was a spark of some kind to kindle the flames of war. Thanks to a couple of phenomena—and his shrewd use of them—Tecumseh got his spark.

Before the Shawnee chief had left the Great Lakes country, the British told him that a comet was due to appear. Then, while traveling south, he apparently felt shivers in the earth that told of massive convulsions to come. By the time he arrived in Took-a-batcha, therefore, he was fully prepared to make his awesome predictions.

Shortly after Tecumseh spoke, a dot of moving light appeared on the Southern horizon. Night by night it grew bigger and brighter until by October 15 it dominated the entire sky, a huge ball of silver fire with a long curving tail.

This light was the famous comet of 1811, visible in Europe as well as in America, its tail estimated by astronomers to be 132 million miles long. The Southern Indians gazed up in open-mouthed awe. There, they were convinced, was Tecumseh's arm of fire.

Later that year the earth began to tremble and shake. There was rumbling as of thunder trapped deep in the earth, but louder than any thunder ever heard before. Lakes emptied. Others were formed. At one point the mighty Mississippi actually reversed its course and flowed north.

The first great shock came on December 11, 1811. The second was five days later. Others came on December 17, and January 23 and February 7 of 1812. The earth truly seemed to be coming to an end. On both sides of the Mississippi, high bluffs slid into the river. With a monstrous roar, huge chasms opened and water rushed in; then the chasms slapped shut, shooting the water up fifty feet or more. The riverbanks for hundreds of miles were littered with the wreckage of flatboats, keelboats, and barges, their cargo, and the bodies of their crew. The river ran thick with foam and driftwood.

Huge holes exploded in the ground, belching water, steam, and gases. Day became as dark as night. For weeks a yellow haze blocked out the sun. In the fields the surface of the earth undulated in waves at about the speed of a trotting horse.

Terrified deer, bear, panthers, and wolves joined the terrified Indians and white settlers on the high ground, pressing close to them, apparently wanting human companionship. All were friends in their greater fear of the convulsing earth.

The tremors came to the Creek Nation out of the northwest. As their homes rocked and forests crashed around them and terrified birds and animals filled the air with their screams, the Creeks ran about in a frenzy. "Tecumseh's back at Tippecanoe!" they yelled. "He's stamping his foot!"

When the shocks finally subsided, the Southern Indians began to mold bullets, perform the Dance of the Lakes, and paint their new war clubs red. The men who were ready to go to war called themselves Red Sticks.

What the country was experiencing was the great earthquake of 1811 and 1812, as violent and long lasting a quake as ever has been recorded. Its center was along the banks of the Mississippi below the mouth of the Ohio. But the tremors spread out in all directions, reaching the Gulf of Mexico and the Atlantic. The earth shook all through 1812, and there were periodic shivers for the next seven years. A common theory on the Southern frontier was that the comet had fallen into the Mississippi and caused the quake.

That so gigantic an occurrence should be so forgotten is one of the many mysteries of American history. This neglect is particularly strange since there were many eyewitnesses who set down their experiences, and the earthquake was a favorite topic of conversation in the United States throughout the duration. Because the area of maximum violence was thinly populated at the time, the loss of life was comparatively small. Today thirteen million Americans live in this region.

Though the Creeks became more and more hostile, small parties raiding isolated cabins on the Southern frontier, they did not go on the warpath in any numbers. Meanwhile, the trouble between the United States and Great Britain had steadily worsened. Finally, the hullabaloo of the frontier could not be denied. President James Madison at last submitted to the pressure and on June 1, 1812, asked Congress to declare war upon Great Britain, which Congress did on June 18.

7

THE
SHAWNEE
POISON

All through 1812 Dale continued to transport white immigrants over the trembling earth to the Mississippi Territory. Toward the end of the year he brought Judge Harry Toulmin and his family to Fort Stoddart on the Tombigbee River, then sent his wagons back to Georgia and rode down to Pensacola alone to see what was happening. In the Florida capital he learned that the Spanish authorities were indeed supplying the Indians with munitions.

On the ride back he ran into a party of mounted white men who had just buried a man named Daly, killed by a Creek raiding party. They urged Dale to return with them to the settlements, but he decided to continue north into the Creek nation and spy upon the Indians.

Hiding in the forest by day and traveling only at

night, he pushed deep into the hostile country. About midnight a few days later he came to the Wolf Path, a noted trail through Creek territory. The night was moonless. His horse snorted nervously. Like his mount, Dale sensed something amiss. Then out of the black somewhere ahead a dog barked.

Dale rode a short distance off the path into the underbrush, dismounted, and crouched behind his horse in case there was shooting. Presently the soft thud of approaching footsteps sounded on the turf, and he stroked his horse to keep him quiet. Judging from the sound, there were a half dozen or so men coming at him through the night.

The footsteps stopped. The men were listening. The only sound was the soft roar of the wind in the forest. Dale stroked his horse. Easily he slipped out his knife from the sheath. He dared not cock his rifle for the telltale click-clock of the hammer.

"He's gone back!" a man yelled.

The language was Creek. There came the rapid patter of moccasined feet as the invisible Indians ran past him and down the path. Dale waited until they were out of earshot, then pressed on through the dark forest, arriving at Sam Manac's stand shortly before daybreak. Manac was a friendly half blood, who operated a crude wilderness inn.

"He informed me that the road was beset," Dale said, "and that it would be difficult to get through. The Shawnee poison had already begun to work. The hostile portion of the Indians were in arms in small parties, murdering friendly Indians and whites."

Dale hid out that day, then rode all night through the white winter mists, reaching Bob Mosely's stand the next dawn. The day was raw. Dale reconnoitered, found nothing suspicious, tethered his horse, and, with the hammer up, entered the cabin. Two Indian boys were warming themselves by the kitchen fire.

Mosely's wife, a niece of the half blood Creek chief Peter McQueen, gave the frontiersman a cup of chicory coffee. As he sat at the table, sipping the strong hot brew, she sent the boys off on an errand. She watched them out of sight, then leaned across the table. "My uncle is going to war against the white people," she said. "He has sworn to kill you on sight for bringing so many settlers into the country."

Dale nodded. Apparently the men who had tried to ambush him the other night were a party of McQueen's braves.

Continuing to travel only at night, the frontiersman reached the settlements on the Alabama River. There he immediately sent a report to Hawkins, telling him what he had seen and heard. Later Dale said:

But he was even then firmly persuaded that the hostilities of the Creeks would only be directed against each other, that it was a war of factions, headed by McQueen on one side and the Big Warrior on the other, and would not be directed against the whites. He appreciated the many noble traits of the Indians, but never understood their perfidy in war, nor the skill with which they can disguise their intentions.

As he went on bringing new settlers into the Mississippi Territory, Dale saw increasing hostility among the Creeks. On July 13, 1813, Sam Manac reported to the frontiersman that a few weeks earlier he had fallen in with a party of Creeks. "An Indian came to me, who goes by the name of High-Headed Jim. He shook hands with me and immediately began to tremble and jerk in every part of his frame, and the very calves of his legs would be convulsed, and he would get entirely out of breath with the agitation."

He was performing the Dance of the Lakes. Thinking that Manac was on the side of the Red Sticks, High Head Jim, as he was usually known, told the half blood that he and the others were on their way to Pensacola to get ammunition from the Spaniards. Upon their return, High Head Jim said, they were going to assault the settlements on the Tombigbee and Alabama Rivers. Other Creeks would attack the Georgians, the Cherokees the Tennesseans, and the Choctaws the settlements on the Mississippi River.

The party of Creeks, about 300 strong, rode south, stopping off on the way to beat up any red men who refused to take the war talk. They burned an Indian village whose inhabitants were friendly to white people. At Burnt Corn Spring they set fire to the cabin of James Cornells, who was absent at the time, and took his wife captive, later trading her to a French woman in Pensacola for a blanket.

Dale, who had given up on the optimistic Hawkins, sent Manac's statement to Colonel James Caller, who commanded the Fifteenth Regiment of Militia, Mississippi Territory. Caller determined to ambush the Creek party on its return from Pensacola and capture the ammunition before the Indians could put it to use. On the border lead was gold. So precious was it that after a skirmish the frontiersmen took the time and trouble to dig out the spent balls that had embedded themselves in the trunks of trees.

Two American spies, David Tate and William Pierce, entered Pensacola and learned that the Indians had received 300 pounds of gunpowder and 600 pounds of lead from Governor Mexco Gonzales Manique in return for a list of Creek towns ready to go on the warpath. Braves in these towns numbered 4800.

In the river settlements of Alabama at this time, according to the United States census of 1810, there were 2000 white men, women, and children. A British fleet was seen off the coast. As the contemporary historian Albert James Pickett wrote, "Everything forboded the extermination of the Americans in Alabama, who were the most isolated and defenseless people imaginable."

The two American spies watched as the Indians performed a war dance in the streets of Pensacola— the equivalent of a formal declaration of war—then stole away to deliver their report.

Colonel Caller marched south with three small companies. On July 25, 1813, he forded the Tombigbee River and was met by Captain Sam Dale with the fifty men he had managed to raise. Others joined the column until the force numbered 180 men—whites, half bloods, and Tory Creeks, as the friendly Indians were called. All were well mounted and heavily armed. Dale carried a double-barreled shotgun, an unusual weapon then.

Caller, wearing a calico hunting shirt and slouch hat, and riding a fine bay horse, led the column forward. The men paddled across the Alabama River in canoes, swimming their horses alongside.

They marched down the Wolf Path and, on July 27, crossed Burnt Corn Creek in what today is Escambia County in southern Alabama. They knew they should be getting close to the Creek party. Dale volunteered to go ahead and reconnoiter with a companion.

Dale told his biographer later:

> My offer was treated lightly. One officer swore that we could 'whip the d----d redskins anywhere, and whip them to h-ll.' I replied, 'Sam Dale can go as near h-ll as any of you. You're on the road there, and may go ahead and be d----d.'

After much debate Caller decided that Dale should push forward with fifteen men, the braggart officer among them. Slowly, cautiously, Dale led his party through the sweet-smelling pine woods. The morning was hot and getting hotter as the sun climbed overhead. Suddenly Dale heard the thudding of hoofs from behind, and the braggart officer galloped around him, apparently taking the frontiersman's caution for cowardice. Dale was infuriated.

"Halt, sir!" he called. "Fall back or I'll blow you

through. On this scout no one goes ahead of me!" He was bluffing, for he was sure they were too close to the Red Sticks to risk a shot. But the braggart officer fell back.

Up ahead was a ring of hills. The men dismounted at the base of them, carefully tethered the mounts, and climbed the steep rise. At last they crawled over the crest. The hills were in a semicircle, overlooking a bend in Burnt Corn Creek. Down through the pines the scouts saw the enemy camp.

The Indians were sitting around their fires, cooking dinner, as their packhorses grazed in the high grass. The Creeks, completely unsuspecting, were not in war paint, had no pickets out, and did not have their weapons close at hand. They could be taken completely by surprise. With a sweep of his arm, Dale motioned to his men to withdraw.

They rode back to the column, and Dale gave his report. Colonel Caller held a quick conference with his officers. They decided to attack at once. Caller split the force into three groups, giving Dale two companies on the left flank.

The column moved forward. At the base of the hills the Americans dismounted. Dale tethered his horse as before, and so did some others, but apparently no regular system was employed. Each man checked his priming and flint, then cocked his weapon. In a wide arc they climbed to the crest. The time was 1 P.M.

"Charge!" Caller shouted.

Yelling, firing, the Americans surged down the hill toward the startled Indians, who jumped up and ran for their weapons. They stood against the charge for a few minutes, then retreated in wild confusion to the thick canebrake along the creek. Dale and some others pursued, tasting the fruits of victory. But most of the American party devoted themselves to capturing and leading off the Red Sticks' packhorses.

Dale drew a bead on a muscular Creek with his shotgun and released one of the triggers. When the smoke cleared, he saw the warrior stretched on the ground. Wanting to have one barrel ready at all times, Dale immediately began to reload. The answering fire from the canebrake was heavy, the smoke rising in a thick white roll.

Next to Dale a man named Elijah Glass was thrown back with a ball through the heart. At the same time Dale felt a sledgehammer blow that sent him staggering. A Red Stick musket ball had hit him in the left side; rolling around his rib, it had lodged in his spine. Dale vomited much blood and felt better. One of his men finished reloading his shotgun for him.

The Creeks, seeing the small number of Americans that confronted them, counterattacked, pushing Dale and the others steadily back.

"Retreat to the hills!" Caller shouted.

He meant to form a line of defense there. But the plundering party heard only the word *retreat* and skedaddled. As frightened as they were, however, they still maintained the presence of mind to drive the packhorses before them, some even mounting the animals in their zeal to save both themselves and the ammunition.

The braggart officer was the first to fly. "I hailed him as he passed," Dale said, "and would have shot him if I could have raised my arm."

Dale, Colonel Caller, and eighty men took a stand in the pine woods at the foot of the hill, but the Creeks pushed them slowly up the hill and down the other side. By then the situation was every man for himself. Someone had taken Dale's horse. He found a pony, dragged himself into the saddle, and started to gallop off when he heard a shout behind him.

A friend of his by the name of Ballard and another man named Lenoir were running through the pines, a party of Creeks in hot pursuit. Dale pulled his mount around and rode back, followed by David Glass, Elijah's brother. Lenoir was sprinting easily over the red carpet of pine needles. But Ballard, who had been shot through the hip, was staggering.

"Save Lenoir!" Dale yelled to Glass. "I'll go to Ballard!"

He galloped forward and was within about fifty yards of him when the Creeks closed in. Ballard jumped around and shot down the foremost Indian, then clubbed his rifle. But the Creeks quickly overwhelmed him.

Meanwhile, Lenoir had jumped up behind Glass, and they rode over to Dale as an Indian leaned down to scalp Ballard.

"If only my gun was loaded!" Glass cried.

"Here's mine with fourteen buckshot in her," Lenoir said. Taking the rifle, Glass rode forward a short distance and fired. The brave with Ballard's scalp pitched forward.

That shot was the last one in the Battle of Burnt Corn, the opening engagement of the bloody Creek War and a disgraceful American defeat. The headlong retreat continued all night. Colonel Caller disappeared. When found fourteen days after the battle, he was wandering in the forest, wearing only his calico hunting shirt and his drawers, completely out of his head. For years the men who had been at Burnt Corn had to endure the ridicule of their neighbors.

Dale was particularly embittered. "(The men) fought bravely," he said, "and but for that unfortunate word 'retreat' they would have annihilated McQueen's party, secured all his supplies, and, in all probability, prevented the war."

8

TERROR
ON
THE
FRONTIER

Dale made his way to Fort Madison, located on a ridge in the forks of the Tombigbee and Alabama Rivers north of Mobile. He suffered so grievously from his wound that he was hardly aware of the panic that seized the entire Southern frontier. Immigration had stopped completely. Communications were cut, the postriders killed, the captured mails sent to the Spanish authorities in Pensacola.

Many families fled, piling children, pigs, and baggage helter-skelter in their wagon, the poultry riding on the oxen. Flatboats filled with other families and their possessions zigzagged down the rivers, the women and children clumsily poling them along as the men stood guard.

Those hardier people who chose to stay came pouring into the stockades, where they were comparatively safe from the Indians, yet highly susceptible to typhus, scarlet fever, and dysentery. Even there, however, panic could come like plague. From Fort Stoddart Judge Toulmin reported, "The people have been fleeing all night."

The Creeks were bound to retaliate for Burnt Corn, but when and where?

Still, no attack came, and as the long drowsy summer days slid by like poured honey and the only smoke was from cooking fires many came to believe that their fears had been groundless. After all, the Indians had badly defeated the Americans at Burnt Corn. Maybe there would be no retaliation.

Meanwhile, a nineteen-year-old Creek chieftain named William Weatherford had taken the war talk. A tall, fair-skinned man with light brown hair, Weatherford was more white man than red man, but his loyalties were entirely with the Creeks. The Indians called him Red Eagle.

He had been at Took-a-batcha, but had not joined the hostile party at that time. Then one day in the summer of 1813 Red Eagle and Sam Manac, returning from a cattle-trading trip in the Mississippi Territory, came upon a group of Red Stick chiefs on Tallewassee Creek, near the Alabama River. The chiefs, who included Peter McQueen, High Head Jim, and Far Off Warrior, were taking the black drink.

According to General Thomas S. Woodward, a half blood contemporary of Weatherford's, in a small book of reminiscences, the Red Stick chiefs told Manac and Red Eagle that they must join the war party or they would be killed. Manac angrily refused to join, leaping upon his horse. One of the Red Sticks, war club upraised, seized the bridle. Manac snatched the weapon from him, banged him on the head, and galloped off.

"Weatherford consented to remain," General Woodward wrote. "He told them that he disapproved of their course, and that it would be their ruin, but that they were his people, he was raised with them, and he would share their fate."

On July 30 Brigadier General Ferdinand L. Claiborne, at the head of 550 United States Army volunteers from Baton Rouge, arrived at Mount Vernon near Fort Madison. A veteran of Fallen Timbers, the great American victory over the red men in the Indiana Territory in 1794, the energetic Claiborne wanted to strike immediately into the heart of the Creek nation.

But Major General Thomas Flourney, commander of Military District Number Seven, which embraced Tennessee, Louisiana, and the Mississippi Territory, was not so energetic. He was afraid that, as soon as the Army went off after the Indians, the Spaniards would attack the Gulf coast. "Your wish to penetrate into the Indian country does not meet my approbation," Flourney wrote Claiborne on August 10. "Our operations must be confined to defensive operations."

Claiborne, the father of Dale's biographer, had no choice but to distribute his command among the various forts along the border. Besides assigning smaller units to the stockades, he sent 150 men under Colonel Joseph Carson to Fort Madison and another 175 under Major Daniel Beasley to Fort Mims, on the south shore of Lake Tensaw in what is now Baldwin County, Alabama.

As senior officer, Beasley took command of the stockade. With the arrival of his troops, Fort Mims had a total of 553 human beings, including American settlers, half bloods, Negroes, and some Spanish refugees from Florida. About a hundred of the civilians were children. The military force was 265.

Like most frontier forts, the stockade at Mims was nearly square, with a blockhouse in one corner, and enclosed about an acre. The palisade, of pine trunks, was twelve feet high with rifle holes cut at intervals. Inside were several log buildings, one of which had an extra palisade around it and was known as the Bastion.

Early in August, Claiborne inspected Fort Mims and ordered Beasley to strengthen the pickets and to build two more blockhouses. This task Beasley failed to do.

On August 23 a Choctaw warrior appeared at Fort Madison and reported that four hundred Indians would attack Fort Easley, a remote and feeble stockade on the Tombigbee, and then would attack Madison. Claiborne marched for Easley with eighty men, having first sent a dispatch to the commanding officer at Mims urging the utmost vigilance.

Contemporary accounts describe Beasley as a brave man. He was also one of the biggest fools in American history. Despite the danger, he let the civilians wander along the lakeshore at will and refused to shut the fort's gates night or day. His dispatches to Claiborne show him to be supremely confident that his garrison —strong by frontier standards—could hold off any number of Indians.

On Sunday, August 29, two breathless Negroes stumbled into the stockade, gasping that a large war party was approaching from the north. It is said that Red Eagle, in command of the Indians, permitted the Negroes to escape so they could alert the fort. Some people think he wanted to avoid widespread bloodshed. At any rate, when the Indians failed to appear, Major Beasley ordered the two men flogged for lying.

Sunday night a Red Stick warrior slipped up to the palisade and whispered through a rifle port to relatives inside that the stockade would be attacked the next day. The relatives ran to Beasley with the information, but he paid no attention.

Monday, August 30, 1813, dawned a beautiful day with a dewy coolness to it. At first light James Cornells, the man whose wife the Creeks had captured at Burnt Corn Spring earlier that summer, mounted his horse and rode north. Soon he came galloping back and drew up at the fort gate.

"Major Beasley," he shouted, "the Indians are coming!"

Beasley was playing cards with some other officers outside his quarters close to the gate. "You just saw a gang of red cattle," he said.

"That gang of red cattle is going to give you a terrible kick before night!" Cornells shouted.

Enraged at what he considered impertinence, Beasley roared, "Arrest that man!" Soldiers ran forward, but Cornells wheeled his horse around and galloped off.

The sun rose in a clear sky and sent slanting shafts of golden light through the dense forest of needle-leafed pine to the east of Mims. The adults in the stockade were as happy and frolicsome as the children. The day before a fresh supply of whisky had arrived; eyewitnesses said Major Beasley was drinking heavily.

That morning he wrote Claiborne: "I have improved the fort at this place and made it much stronger than when you were here. I was much pleased with the appearance of my men yesterday when it was expected every moment that the Indians would appear. They very generally seemed anxious to see them."

He added a note assuring his commanding officer of his ability "to maintain the fort against any number of Indians."

Dark eyes in the forest watched the dispatch carrier ride out and away. The hour was approaching noon. Beasley and his officers were still playing cards. The soldiers were about to eat dinner. One of the Negroes who had reported the Indians the day before was tied up for his flogging. The girls and young men were dancing to a gourd fiddle, and the children were sporting from tent to cabin inside the palisade. The drums beat to dinner.

"Indians!"

A thousand Creek warriors came sprinting across the sand toward the open gate. When sighted, they were just thirty paces away. Major Beasley leaped to his feet and ran to shut the gate. But it had been left open so long that the winds had swept up the sand around it. It wouldn't budge. As Beasley struggled with it, a Creek broke his foolish head with a war club.

Red Eagle in the lead, the painted warriors poured through the gate. They killed and scalped the Negro who was tied up to be flogged. They killed and scalped the Spaniards as they knelt, praying. The soldiers fought with the courage of desperation, but with the Indians all inside the palisade there was no chance whatever.

Some soldiers climbed on cabin roofs in the enclosure and kept up a rapid fire from there. The Indians set the cabins ablaze with flaming arrows. The soldiers continued their fire until the burning cabins collapsed under them.

In other parts of the fort the women loaded the rifles for the men and, when they fell, fought on themselves until they too fell. A huge Negro wielding an ax accounted for many Indians until he at last went down, surrounded by the bodies of his assailants.

The cry went up, "To the Bastion! To the Bastion!"

The survivors ran to the little palisade, where they were jammed together like cattle in a slaughter pen, too tightly packed to defend themselves as the Red Sticks closed in. The day was filled with flames, smoke, screams, and horror.

Red Eagle tried frantically, but in vain, to get his braves to spare the women and children. Sickened by the butchery, he left the scene early. "My warriors," he told Dale years later, "were like famished wolves, and the first taste of blood made their appetites insatiable." The work went on until 5 P.M.

The Fort Mims massacre was the last Indian attack on a settlement east of the Mississippi and the worst of any. Of the 553 inside the fort 36 survived. They included a few half bloods who were made prisoner, some Negroes kept for slaves, and 15 people who cut their way through the palisade and escaped. One of these lucky ones was Dr. Thomas G. Holmes, who later described the event to the historian Pickett.

Also among the survivors were Mrs. Vicey McGirth and her daughters. About fifteen years earlier, an orphaned Indian boy named Sanota had come to the McGirth cabin, asking for something to eat. The McGirths, who had no son, adopted the boy. When he grew to manhood he had returned to his tribe and later had joined the Red Sticks. He was among the warriors at Fort Mims.

Toward the end of the day, he came upon Mrs. McGirth and his foster sisters. Mad with blood, he was about to tomahawk them when he saw who they were. He thrust them into a corner and fought off all the warriors who tried to kill them.

McGirth had been away from the fort at the time of

the attack. He returned that night and had the ghastly experience of searching through the piles of burned and mutilated dead for the bodies of his wife and children. Though he couldn't find them, he assumed they had been killed. Afterward, in his grief, he volunteered for the most desperate missions. Months after the massacre, the McGirths had a joyous reunion in Mobile. Sanota was later killed in the war.

For some reason, perhaps because of sheer exhaustion, the Red Sticks left their own slain on the field. The white burial party that arrived ten days later counted 109 dead Indians, including Far Off Warrior. Another 50 Creeks were reported to have died of their wounds at Burnt Corn Spring, where the war party retired after the attack.

At sunset August 31, Nah-hee, a Tory Creek, returned to Fort Madison from a scout and reported to Dale the fall of Fort Mims. Nah-hee said he had also spotted a large body of Red Sticks under the Prophet Francis close by.

When the news spread, Fort Madison was loud with the shrieks of the women and children. Even veteran frontiersmen grew pallid. But Dale and the other officers managed to calm everyone down, and they prepared the garrison to defend the fort against the expected attack. It did not come. Apparently the Red Sticks decided the fort was too well guarded.

The terror on the frontier continued to mount. An English schooner was reported to have put into Pensacola, loaded with arms and ammunition for the Red

Sticks. The British were offering five dollars for every American scalp. Settlers began to flee around the clock, abandoning all their possessions. The Southern sky was filled with pillars of smoke as the Red Sticks burned the cabins. They drove off the cattle and sent the pigs into the cornfields to fatten them for the victory feasts in the fall.

On the afternoon of September 1 a war party fell upon the cabin of the Ransom Kimbell family on Bassett's Creek, killing twelve women and children. One of the scalped women, Mrs. Sarah Merril, was revived by a rain that fell that night. In the dark she searched through the bodies until she found her one-year-old son, whose short hair had saved him from being scalped. She carried him through the forest to Fort Sinquefield, about a mile west. Both mother and child survived.

Next day a party from the fort went to the Kimbell farm, loaded the bodies into an ox cart, and brought them back to Sinquefield for burial. About noon, as the funeral services were drawing to a close, an old man remarked upon a big "flock of wild turkeys" coming from the south. A younger person followed his pointing finger.

"Those aren't turkeys, they're Indians!" he yelled.

"Indians!" The fearful cry spread. The war party, about a hundred Red Sticks under the Prophet Francis, wore a band of turkey feathers in their hair and were advancing bent over. At the shout of alarm, they straightened up and raced to cut off the members of the burial party, who were running for the fort.

Then, seeing that they were too late to catch them, the Indians turned upon a group of women who had been washing at the spring at the foot of the hill. The women were running up the hill, one of them still carrying an iron washpot on her head. The Indians quickly closed the distance. The women appeared to be lost.

Then, on the spot, a young man named Isaac Hayden conceived a daring plan. Leaping upon a horse, he whistled up the dogs in the fort and, with all sixty of them bounding and barking behind him, galloped down the hill toward the Indians.

The dogs hurled themselves upon the red men, who were forced to stop their pursuit of the women and to protect themselves against the snarling pack. In the savage fight the dogs tore the throat out of a number of Creeks, but many of them were killed. The rest of them, terrified by the racket of battle, ran into the forest, and only a few were ever recovered. Nevertheless, Hayden's Dogs of War became famous on the Southern frontier.

Seeing a Creek with tomahawk upraised over a woman, Hayden galloped forward, pulling a pistol from his saddle holster, and shot the warrior dead. The woman ran on and reached the fort safely. Another woman, Winnie Odom, collapsed before she got to the gate. A soldier ran down the hill, grabbed her by the hair, and thus dragged her into the fort. Only one woman, Mrs. Sarah Phillips, was killed.

With the Indians' bullets droning around him, Hayden galloped back to the fort. As he entered the gate, his horse fell with a bullet crease in the neck. The rider was uninjured, though five bullet holes were counted in his clothes. He and the others managed to beat off the Red Stick attack.

Fearing another attack, the people at Sinquefield fled through the forest that night to Fort Madison, ten miles south. With the newcomers, there were a thousand persons crowded into the small stockade.

Early one morning a young man named Jeremiah Austill arrived at Fort Madison after a daring ride through the hostile country with a dispatch from General Flourney. The dispatch was intended only to alert the fort, but it was ambiguously worded. Colonel Carson and Dale took it to be an order to abandon the stockade.

Both men were appalled. Madison protected one of the principal settlements west of the Alabama. Reluctantly, Carson obeyed the order as he understood it. Most of the settlers prepared to leave with him.

"As his drum beat for his men to march," Dale said, "I beat mine for volunteers, being determined to remain if I could get ten men to stand by me." As the last of the Army marched out of the fort, Dale marched in with fifty men and their families.

Dale and Jeremiah Austill's father, Captain Evan Austill, who had also decided to remain, directed the settlers in the defense of the fort. They built a fence around the fort of sharpened stakes slanting outward and thickly plastered the blockhouses with clay as a preventative against being burned by the Creek fire arrows.

There were not enough men to set out pickets at night. Dale and Austill improvised beacons of lightwood that stood on clay-covered platforms atop fifty-foot poles on each side of the fort and threw a brilliant light for a hundred yards around. Fresh fuel was raised to the platforms by means of chains.

The frontiersmen, accustomed to hunting deer at night by shining a light into their eyes, were deadly marksmen at this type of shooting. After a number of braves had been shot in the head trying to slip up to the fort at night, the Red Sticks kept their distance.

But Dale knew that the dark eyes were out there and watching. He had the women wear men's clothes and carry a rifle during the day to give an exaggerated notion of the garrison's strength.

General Flourney sent Dale a note, advising him to pull out since he was certain to be attacked by an overwhelming force of Indians. "I sent him back a reply," the frontiersman told his biographer, "saying I had a gallant set of boys and if the General heard of the fall of Fort Madison he would find a pile of (copper) hides to tan."

9

THE
GREAT
CANOE
BATTLE

The Red Sticks did not attack Fort Madison, but as the long year stretched into the fall they continued to burn the abandoned cabins along the frontier and to ambush small parties. Though still suffering from the wound received at Burnt Corn, Dale got permission from Colonel Carson to make a counterattack. The frontiersman was given a force of thirty Mississippi Volunteers and forty militiamen from Clarke County, Alabama.

During the second week of November, Nah-hee came back from a scout on the east side of the Alabama River and told Dale he had seen a party of about eighty Red Sticks camped there. The frontiersman and his force promptly set out afoot, marching over earth that still quivered from the earthquake. They passed a number of abandoned farms, the buildings in ashes, hogs feasting in the cornfields, but saw no Indians.

The second day they crossed the river in two canoes that Dale had earlier hidden in the dense canebrake. They spent the night on the east bank. The night was cold and the men were lightly clad, but Dale could not let them light fires for fear of giving away their position.

With dawn next day they resumed the march up-river. Dale ordered the two canoes manned and had them keep pace with the force he led along the river-bank. The canoes, he reasoned, would be useful if the men had to cross the river in a hurry or if there were wounded to be carried.

The white men had gone a short distance when they saw two Indian dugouts paddling toward them. The Indians spotted them at the same time and quickly reversed course, disappearing around a bend in the river.

"Follow me!" Dale yelled.

The men ran forward, each cocking his rifle. Soon Dale and a scout named George Foster were about one hundred yards ahead of the others, running through a cage of thick, rattling cane ten feet high or more. The soft, wet ground deadened their footsteps. The path made a sharp turn to the right. Dale and Foster came upon a group of five painted Red Sticks, walking toward them in single file.

The leader raised his rifle, and so did Dale. Both gave an exclamation of surprise. The Creek was the frontiersman's old friend, Bill Milfort. Before Milfort could fire, Dale shot him dead. Foster shot the next in line. The other three crashed into the canebrake. Dale was deeply sorry about having to kill Milfort. "I often bewail the destiny that doomed him to fall by the hand of his best friend," he said. "Such are the dreadful necessities of war. Some time after I sought and interred his fleshless bones. They now moulder on the banks of the river he loved so well."

The white party, afloat and ashore, continued up the river to Random's Landing, on a beautiful bend of the Alabama in what is now Monroe County. Suddenly Dale and his men emerged from the cane onto a broad field. A tenseness was in the air. Many fires were burning under scaffolds for drying meat. Obviously a large group of Indians had just decamped, though none could be found in the area. The experience was eerie.

The men re-entered the cane on the other side of the field, continuing upriver. Then the path petered out. Dale began to ferry his men across to the west bank, where the going was easier. All had crossed but Dale and twelve others. This party dug up some wild sweet potatoes and built a fire to roast them for a late breakfast. It was shortly after ten o'clock on the cool, sunny morning of November 12, 1813. (Dale's biographer says November 13, but later historians contradict him.)

"Indians!"

The cry came across the river from the western bank. Dale saw a huge canoe filled with Red Sticks moving swiftly down the river toward them, paddles flashing in the morning sun. The Indians apparently meant to land at a canebrake just above Dale's group.

"Come on!" Dale yelled, sprinting for the cane. Only seven of his men managed to stay with him. They came puffing up just as the Red Sticks were about to land. Eleven of them, a chief and ten braves, were in the canoe. The Indians did not appear to have seen the white men. Two warriors jumped into the water to guide the craft to shore. The river ran with foaming swiftness; its thick musty smell was strong.

Dale and James Smith each shouldered his rifle. The two explosions sounded as one. Both Indians, drilled through the head, were hurled back by the impact of the bullet, and their bodies began to float downstream. Rapidly chopping with their short paddle, the other Creeks propelled their craft into deep water.

The canoe was a dugout made out of a cypress log. Used ordinarily for hauling corn, it was thirty feet long, had a three-foot beam, and its sides were several inches thick—thick enough to stop a rifle ball.

The chief gave a soft command. Three warriors rolled into the water on the far side of the dugout and began to work it out of the range of the white men's rifles as the other Indians lay in the bottom of the canoe.

The Americans' fire had no effect. For faster loading, Dale and the others each took a handful of rifle balls from their shot bag and put them in their mouth. One of the swimmers kept rising up to yell to Red

Eagle, who apparently was somewhere close by, "Yos-ta-hah! Yos-ta-hah! They're ruining us!"

Each time he rose up, the white men fired—and missed. After several volleys, while the Americans were reloading, the warrior hauled himself up chest-high and asked politely in perfect English, "Why don't you shoot me?"

Grimly Dale filled the powder horn measure and poured the coarse black grains down the brown octagonal barrel of his rifle. He took a greased buck-skin patch from the hinged box in the stock, spat a ball into it, and drove the two home with the ramrod. He pushed the frizzen of the lock up and back, poured the fine black priming powder from his smaller horn into the priming pan, and snapped the frizzen closed.

Next time the swimmer showed himself, Dale held his fire. The bullets of the other rifles kicked up the water behind the brave or thwacked harmlessly into the side of the dugout, which by then had reached midstream; the strong current was sweeping it away.

Dale raised his rifle. The long, heavy barrel stead-ied and held. Allowing for wind, the frontiersman drew a bead on a spot between the brave's hands clutching the gunwale and waited. The bright brass front sight edged down into the dark V of the rear sight. The brave rose up.

"Why . . .?" he asked.

Dale gentled the delicate trigger. The eagle head of the hammer pecked forward, the flint struck sparks on the frizzen, the priming charge hissed, and the rifle shoved into his shoulder. The explosion made a long, whiplash crack that echoed over the water. Instantly the brave lay back with a bullet in his brains.

The other two swimmers slid over the side into the dugout and lay with the others in the bottom. They were getting away. Both American canoes were on the other side of the river.

"Bring over the boats!" Dale yelled.

At once eight of his men jumped into a big canoe and paddled out to the drifting dugout. They had not seen all the action and seemed to think the Indians were dead. The man in the bow grabbed the dugout's gunwale and peered inside.

"Live Indians!" he cried. "Back water, boys! Back water!" The frightened men pushed back to the west bank. The Indians sat upright in the dugout and began to ply the paddle.

Frantically Dale searched the opposite bank. His blood was up, he was hot with the fire of impending combat, but how to get to it? His eye lit on Caesar, a free Negro, sitting in a little pirogue about a hundred yards below the Indians' dugout. "Caesar!" the frontiersman yelled. "Bring your boat over!"

The Negro hesitated. He had just seen eight well-armed white men fleeing from the dugout. Dale shook his rifle. "Caesar, I swear I'll shoot you if you don't bring that pirogue over here!"

Caesar paddled across. Dale, James Smith, and Jerry Austill ran down the musty bank and climbed into the pirogue. The little craft would hold no more.

So three frontiersmen, accompanied by a Negro noncombatant, went out into the Alabama River to meet nine powerful Creek warriors. The great Canoe Battle, one of the most savage and unique combats in the long bloody history of the American frontier, was about to begin.

Along the border there were many desperate hand-to-hand battles between the white men and the red men. Most of them, however, were fought without spectators in the forest gloom, like the encounters of wild beasts, and we have only the understandably colored word of the winners, the survivors, that they took place at all. But in the case of the Canoe Battle fifty-nine Americans on one bank and nine on the other, as well as a certain number of Indians hidden in the cane, witnessed the fight. The incident is well documented. Austill also left an account of it, which agrees substantially with Dale's and the others. In such a wildly confused action, there are bound to be minor discrepancies.

On land, all things being equal, the Americans usually won over the Indians in hand-to-hand fighting. On water, however, the Southern Indians excelled. Furthermore, in this instance, the Americans, outnumbered three to one, were in a wobbly little pirogue that might overturn with the slightest mismove while the Indians were in a big stable dugout. Dale, then forty-one years old, was still seriously hampered by his old wound. Smith was a stocky Georgian of twenty-five; he had already killed several Indians in personal combat. Tall, rawboned Jerry

Austill from South Carolina, the youth who had
brought the supposed evacuation order to Fort Madison, was just nineteen. But all three had the paramount characteristic of the frontiersman: supreme
self-confidence.

Rapidly the dugout bore down upon them as the
eager Indians paddled through the flat, brown water.
They were naked but for a loincloth. The chief, who
sat in the bow, wore a panther-skin headdress. He and
his warriors were heavily tattooed, and all were wearing war paint. Each face was black, eyes encircled
with red; their arms, legs, and chest were striped in
red, black, white, and yellow. The distance closed to
forty yards.

"Let's give 'em a broadside," Dale said, wanting to
whittle down the odds. Each of the three Americans
leveled his rifle and released the trigger. Three small
puffs of white smoke drifted across the water. All
three weapons had misfired. The odds remained the
same.

"Bring us alongside," Dale ordered Caesar, club-
bing his rifle. At twenty yards, a striped, muscular
arm in the dugout cocked back and snapped forward.
Something flashed in the sun. Dale had no time to
dodge or protect himself. The missile, a scalping
knife, pierced the thin side of the pirogue and grazed
his thigh.

When the boats were ten feet apart, the chief, who
had recognized the frontiersman, yelled in English,
"Now for it, Big Sam!"

The boats bumped. Caesar held them clamped together. Dale jumped up, putting one foot in the Indian dugout. The closest Red Stick aimed his musket at him and pulled the trigger. There was a sharp hiss and a puff of smoke as the weapon flashed in the pan. The warrior clubbed the musket and swung at Dale's head. The frontiersman parried the blow with his own rifle then swung himself. Skull broken, the Indian toppled into the river.

The chief pointed a rifle at Austill. Austill swung at him with an oar. The chief dodged the blow, then slammed his weapon down on the young man's head. Austill fell, sprawled across the two boats. The chief raised his rifle to finish him off.

Dale and Smith struck together. The chief fell heavily, his head crushed under the panther-skin headdress. Dale had swung so hard that his rifle had broken off at the lock. He hurled the stock at the nearest Indian.

Almost blinded by blood, Austill staggered to his feet. A warrior decked him with a roundhouse swing of his war club. Austill, a youth with a remarkably hard head, once more regained his feet. Grappling with the warrior, he snatched the war club from him, bashed in his head, and knocked him into the river.

Smith downed two braves in quick succession. One lay still. The other crawled off to the bow of the dugout. Dale, weaponless, glanced about for something with which to continue the fight.

"Here, Big Sam!" Caesar yelled, handing up his musket, bayonet attached. To do so, however, he had to let go of the dugout. The two boats began to drift apart. The frontiersman, still with one foot in each craft, felt as if he were being torn in two. Dale, the insatiable combatant, leaped into the dugout.

He stood with legs widespread in the Indian boat, facing the stern. Two Red Sticks lay dead at his feet. One of Smith's Indians lay behind him in a dazed condition. In front of him were four braves, in excellent condition. Out of the corner of his eye, the frontiersman saw Caesar trying to maneuver the pirogue with a broken paddle, while Smith and Austill each hurriedly reprimed his rifle. He could hear a monotonous *snap-snap-snap*. The dazed warrior behind him was trying to shoot him with a pistol, but the piece kept misfiring.

Except for the chief's challenge and Caesar's yell, not a word had been spoken on either side. There was nothing to say. The pistol kept snapping behind his back. Dale chose to take the chance that it would continue to misfire and to concentrate on the four braves facing him. Wide as the dugout was, they could not fight him together. He would be able to take them on one by one.

The first warrior charged forward, swinging his musket at Dale's face. The frontiersman parried, twisted to one side, and drove his bayonet up to the hilt into the Indian's chest. The warrior went down. The second one came on.

The bayonet was stuck. Frantically Dale tried to yank it out as the other warrior rushed him, tomahawk high. There was nothing Dale could do. There was no time even to jump into the river. The toma-

hawk flashed in the sun. Then the warrior grunted, falling, and the long, loud, reverberating bang of a rifle came across the water. Austill had managed to reprime. Finally then Dale was able to free his bayonet. The third warrior charged—and got the bayonet.

Only the dazed brave, who never had stopped trying to fire his pistol, and the fourth warrior were left. Dale knew this mighty Creek well. He was Tar-cha-chee, a famous wrestler and the best ballplayer of his clan. He paused, waiting for Dale to come to him. Dale stood still, gasping for breath.

Tar-cha-chee stepped back to the very tip of the dugout. He began to tremble and jerk, doing the Dance of the Lakes. Then he gave his war whoop and yelled, "Big Sam! Tar-cha-chee is a man! I am coming —come on!"

With a wild scream, he came bounding over the bodies of his tribesmen, swinging his musket at Dale's head. The frontiersman parried, hands stinging from the force of the blow. Tar-cha-chee's musket glanced off the barrel of Dale's gun and slammed down upon his left shoulder, instantly dislocating it.

Sick with pain, the frontiersman still managed to twist his torso about and jab the bayonet into the warrior. The bayonet slid around a rib and stuck in Tar-cha-chee's back. The thrust carried Dale forward, and he fell heavily upon the Indian. Dale struggled to free the bayonet, now unwieldy with the weight of the musket above it, as the warrior fought to raise himself.

"Tar-cha-chee is a man," he gasped. "He's not afraid to die!"

Dale worried the bayonet out and at once slipped it into the brave's heart. Then, smeared with war paint and blood, he got to his feet and turned to face the Indian in the bow, who was still trying to fire his pistol.

The Creek gave his war whoop and yelled, "I am a warrior! I'm not afraid to die!" He got the bayonet.

Gingerly, Dale sat down on the gunwale. The entire action had lasted just ten minutes. Of the nine Indians in the dugout, Dale, alone, had accounted for five, sharing with Smith the dispatch of the chief.

Caesar at last managed to bring the pirogue back alongside with the broken paddle. Smith and Austill climbed into the dugout, their eyes widening at the gory sight. One by one they lifted the dead Indians by the shoulders and ankles and tossed them into the river, the white men on both banks cheering with each splash.

Dale sat quietly, holding his shoulder, getting no satisfaction from the cheers. He was very tired and rather sad.

Suddenly a cry came from the men on the east bank of the river. "Weatherford's coming!" Dale ferried his party over to the west bank, and everyone got back to Fort Madison safely.

Later Dale asked Weatherford, Red Eagle, why he hadn't come to the assistance of his warriors during the Canoe Battle. "He said he had no boats," the frontiersman told his biographer, "and we were beyond the range of his guns; that he supposed I had a hundred men below prepared for battle; that he had but thirty warriors; that he had made a circuit of three miles and ambushed his force in a canebrake, intending to attack us as we marched down the river, which I had defeated by crossing my men immediately over from Random's Landing."

10

RED
EAGLE'S
LEAP

At Fort Madison a doctor set Dale's shoulder. General
Claiborne sent word asking the frontiersman to attend
a council of officers at Point Jackson on the Tombigbee River. The meeting was to decide whether to
build a fort at Weatherford's Bluff on the east bank of
the Alabama River, where Red Eagle kept his supplies of cattle and corn that were so essential to the
Red Sticks.

Claiborne's large tent was filled with neatly uni-
formed officers. Among those attending was Pushmataha, the great chief of the Choctaws, who was
fighting with five hundred of his best braves on the
side of the United States. Dale had the highest respect for Pushmataha and fully appreciated the effect
of his loyalty to the Americans.

"Had the Choctaws taken up arms against us," he

said, "in less than thirty days the whole country from the Tombigbee to the Mississippi would have been steeped in blood."

Fortunately for the Americans, the other Indian tribes did not join Tecumseh's proposed confederation, for the simple reason that they could not get along together. The Creeks fought alone.

In reward for his loyalty, Pushmataha had been made a brigadier general in the United States Army. Resplendent in his new blue uniform with gold epaulets, sword, silver spurs, and plumed hat, the Choctaw chief sat silently as the white officers around him argued the issue. The prevalent opinion was that the proposed fort would be too near the enemy and therefore too dangerous.

Dale, taciturn by nature and self-conscious about his lack of formal education, sat well in the back of the tent, letting the others—most of whom were strangers to him—do the talking. At last Claiborne looked up from his table and sought out the frontiersman.

"What do you think, Captain Dale?"

The others twisted about as Dale arose, giving a murmur of surprise at his wild appearance. The frontiersman was gaunt and haggard. His buckskins were frayed, tanned by the smoke of a thousand campfires. He wore a bearskin cap and carried a long rifle. His big knife hung by his shot bag. Calmly, he let his eyes sweep the crowd.

"General," he drawled, "there's so many shining buttons here to dazzle a fellow's eyes, I don't know whether the opinion of a frontier man will be listened to. But I have one favor to ask of you."

"Name it."

"Sir, have the women and children now in my charge at Fort Madison brought here, and I'll be damned if *I* don't build the fort—and keep it after it's built."

Claiborne strode back and forth in the tent a few times, then whirled and said, "Captain Dale, let's take a glass of grog."

The frontiersman came forward and the two drank together. Claiborne put down his empty glass, turning to the council. "Gentlemen," he said, "the point is decided. We must build the fort. At all hazards it must be built. General Jackson is advancing, and supplies must be secured for him."

The Creek War was coming to a head. The previous month Andrew Jackson had crossed the Tennessee River into the present state of Alabama with 5000 Tennessee militia and nearly 1000 Indian allies to attack the Red Stick towns. But he had written that he feared famine more than Indians.

Before leaving for Weatherford's Bluff, General Claiborne asked Dale to take his scouts and join with a party of Pushmataha's braves in reconnoitering both banks of the Alabama. The party came back to report the way clear.

On November 17, Claiborne's troops rafted across the river and within less than two weeks had built a stockade with a half-moon battery that commanded the river. The position was named Fort Claiborne in honor of the general. The troops rounded up a big herd of Weatherford's cattle and filled the stockade with the Red Stick leader's corn to feed Jackson's men when they arrived.

About 120 miles above Fort Claiborne, on a bluff along the south bank of the Alabama River, as it swings east, in what is now Lowndes County, Alabama, was the town of Ikana chaka, the Holy Ground. It was Red Eagle's headquarters and the chief center of the fanatic element of the Indians. Captives were taken there to be burned at the stake.

Creek and Shawnee prophets called it "the grave of white men." They had inscribed magic circles around its borders, assuring their followers that, if the white men dared to trespass, the earth would open up and swallow them. No trails led to the Holy Ground. The surrounding territory was dense forest, canebrake, and swamp.

This town Claiborne determined to attack. By then the nasty Southern winter had set in. Most of the men were without heavy clothing. Many had no blankets or even shoes.

The operation was considered so dangerous that twenty-six of Claiborne's officers (Dale was not among them) signed a petition, urging the general to abandon his project. But when Claiborne gave the order to march, they all marched—even those whose term of service had expired. On December 13 the column, nearly a thousand strong, trooped out of Fort

Claiborne, the band playing "Over the Hills and Far Away."

After several days' march, Claiborne halted to build a stockade called Fort Deposit, where he left his wagons, cannon, baggage, and sick with a garrison of a hundred men. On the morning of December 22 the army resumed the march through the wilderness and late that afternoon made camp ten miles from the Holy Ground.

The men were tired, cold, and wet. They had not tasted meat for eight days, subsisting entirely on parched corn. But Claiborne ordered the attack for noon the next day. The troops ate their meager meal, then settled down to get what rest they could on the cold ground, huddling together in two's and three's to take advantage of each other's body warmth. Dale and the others with blankets shared them with those not so fortunate.

The night was still except for the wearisome dripping of frigid water from the trees and sky. It seemed utterly unending. At long last a solitary bird called out, then fell silent. Still later all the birds in the forest suddenly exploded into song.

The dark blue of the sky gave way to a smutty gray, then a paler gray, and the great black trees emerged from the gloom, apparently floating in the thick ground fog. The men arose, stretching stiff muscles and griping, as veterans do, in the salty manner that has nothing to do with a lack of morale. Uncomfortable troops make the best fighters. Still griping, they ate their parched-corn breakfast. As a pale sun came slowly up in a leaden sky, they broke camp, formed a column, and marched briskly through the forest, sparkling white with frost, toward the Holy Ground.

Just before noon, about two miles from the Indian stronghold, Claiborne signaled a halt and divided his army into three forces to surround the town. Dale was assigned to the left column, composed of a battalion of militia along with Pushmataha and 150 of his braves.

Quickly but cautiously the men moved through the forest. Although the sun was nearly overhead, it gave no warmth, and the day was sour. Approaching the outskirts of the town, Dale's column formed in line of battle and, all abreast with a space of about six feet between each man, pressed forward. Rifles cocked, they came to a picket fence, expecting momentarily to receive a fusillade. But the fence was not manned.

Farther on they approached a long, low wall of lightwood. The prophets had assured the warriors that if a white army ever tried to attack the town, they would fire this consecrated fuel and all the invaders would be consumed in the flames. But no prophet was around, and the attacking force passed over the wall without incident. The same was true of the magic circles inscribed in the ground outside the town.

Red Eagle, who put no more stock in the claims of his religious men than did the white men, had that morning sent the women and children of the town to the dense woods across the Alabama. The only occupants of the Holy Ground at noon on December 23 were the prophets and the Red Sticks.

As the American army neared the town the men could hear the booming of the Creek war drums and the frenzied screams of the prophets. But they could see none of the enemy. Ahead was a stream. The Americans started to wade across it. Suddenly on the opposite bank a large body of Creek gunmen rose up and gave the attackers a volley. Behind them the Creek bowmen sent flight after humming flight of shafts into the American line. The attackers splashed across the stream, firing as they ran.

Amid the bowmen was a Shawnee prophet who ran back and forth, waving a cow's tail in each hand and shrieking wildly. The religious men had told the Creeks that they were impervious to any white man's bullet, that the ball would split in two when it struck their charmed chest. A Mississippi Territory Volunteer named Gatlin, resting his rifle against a tree, drew a bead on the prophet and squeezed the trigger. The Shawnee fell with a bullet through the heart.

The Red Sticks stared down at him in dismay. The prophets had lied! Confidence shattered, the Creeks broke and ran despite all of Red Eagle's efforts to rally them. Because of the difficult terrain the American army had not managed to surround the town completely. Hundreds of Creeks made their escape by paddling canoes or swimming across the Alabama River.

Last to leave the Holy Ground was the Red Stick

leader. Finding himself hedged in on three sides by the rapidly advancing Americans, Red Eagle sprang upon his magnificent gray stallion, Arrow, and rode up to the bluff overlooking the river.

Dale watched, leaning on his rifle, as Red Eagle paused on the edge of the bluff and gazed down into the swirling muddy water, oblivious to the bullets that moaned around him. The frontiersman knew what was in Red Eagle's mind. The young chief trotted his mount back about thirty strides, then turned his head toward the bluff. With a nudge of his heels and a ringing "Ho ya!" Red Eagle urged the mighty stallion forward.

Hoofs thundering on the turf, Arrow galloped to the edge of the bluff, then leaped up and out. In the sudden hush, horse and rider looked like one being, stretched against the sullen gray sky, before they began slowly to fall. Hitting the water with a great brown splash, Arrow began to swim across the wide river with powerful strokes as bullets from a hundred rifles—Dale's not among them—kicked up spurts all around him.

Red Eagle never lost his seat. Miraculously none of the bullets hit him or his stallion. On the opposite bank, he brandished his rifle, shouted defiantly, and galloped into the forest. That escape was Red Eagle's leap, one of the most celebrated deeds in the history of the Southern frontier.

The Battle of the Holy Ground was over. Behind them the Creeks had left thirty-three dead. How many had been wounded could not be known since

the Red Sticks had carried them all off. American casualties numbered twenty-one.

The importance of a battle, however, is not measured in the amount of blood spilled. As Dale said, "The moral effect of this bold movement into the heart of the nation, upon ground held sacred and impregnable, was great. It taught the savages that they were neither inaccessible nor invulnerable; it destroyed their confidence in their prophets, and it proved what volunteers, even without shoes, clothing, blankets, or provisions, would do for their country."

In Red Eagle's lodge, the Americans discovered a letter to the chief from Mexco Manique, the Spanish governor at Pensacola, complimenting him for the great success of the attack on Fort Mims. They also found in the center of the square a tall pole from which dangled the hundreds of scalps taken at Mims, the soft hair of infants and the white hair of old men.

Pickett wrote that the Americans arrived just in time to rescue Mrs. Sophia Durant and several other friendly half bloods, who were bound to stakes in the square with lightwood piled around them. Other nineteenth century historians cast doubt upon the matter. Dale made no mention of it in his memoirs.

The Americans set fire to the Holy Ground's two hundred cabins, then moved out, laying waste the countryside. Christmas dinner was parched corn and boiled acorns. Five days later they staggered into Fort Claiborne, weary, feverish, starved, but victorious.

*   *   *

On February 1, 1814, General Claiborne took his army on another expedition into the Creek nation, this operation aimed at Old Towns on the Cahaba River. The Red Sticks knew the Americans were coming; the invaders found the towns deserted, completely stripped of food, blankets, and anything else that might be of use to them. By this time they had exhausted their parched corn.

A keelboat loaded wth provisions was scheduled to meet the army, but did not appear. The men were weak with hunger. Three Americans went to search for the keelboat. The Indians tomahawked two; the third escaped to tell the story.

The army had no choice but to pull back. On the return march to Fort Claiborne the troops lived on acorns, hickory nuts, and rats. To get the rats, the soldiers set fire to the Indian cabins and bayoneted them as they scurried out.

"I saw one soldier offer two dollars for a rat," Dale said. "The offer was rejected. The owner demanded ten dollars." Rat is said to be quite good, tasting like chicken.

The abortive expedition proved too much for Claiborne, who died shortly after his return from Old Towns.

Weakened by exposure, Dale suffered a severe infection of his old wound. At Fort Claiborne Dr. Neal Smith removed the musket ball that had been in the frontiersman's spine and ruining his health since the Battle of Burnt Corn more than six months earlier.

Dale was slow to recover. A number of other bloody battles were fought as the Americans pursued a course of extermination, but for Dale the war was over.

11

DALE'S
RIDE

On March 27, 1814, Jackson attacked a force of a thousand Red Sticks at Tohopeka, or Horseshoe Bend, on the Tallapoosa River. At Horseshoe Bend the Creeks made their last stand. Fighting from behind log ramparts, they stood fast against the American frontal assault. But a force of six hundred Cherokees and Tory Creeks swam the river and attacked from the rear. The Red Stick defense soon fell apart.

"It is believed," Jackson wrote in his battle report, "that not more than twenty have escaped."

Red Eagle was not present at Horseshoe Bend. Seeing that further resistance was suicidal, he rode Arrow into Jackson's camp and begged for peace. The treaty was signed on August 9, 1814. In the last of the many wars between the red man and the white man east of the Mississippi, more Indians had been killed than in any earlier conflict.

The once-mighty Creek nation was destroyed. Old Sharp Knife, as the Indians called Jackson, forced the Creeks to cede twenty-three million acres of their land—one fifth of what today is Georgia and three fifths of Alabama—to the United States. The Red Sticks were annihilated.

Of Weatherford, Dale said, "He fought like a hero, and with great military tact, until his towns were burned, his country ravaged, and his warriors slain; when moved by starving women and children all around him, he surrendered. . . ."

After the war Weatherford moved to the white settlements near Montgomery, Alabama, and married Mary Stiggins, a white girl. Dale was his best man.

Weatherford had once been wealthy, but the war ruined him just as it did his nation. He told Dale that "his old comrades, the hostiles, ate his cattle from starvation; the peace party ate them from revenge; and the squatters because he was a d——d redskin. 'So,' said he, 'I have come to live among gentlemen.' "

Jackson was particularly anxious to bring the Creeks to peace since he had heard that the British had landed troops in Pensacola and were furnishing supplies to the Indians. During November, 1814, he made a forced march to the Spanish capital and, in a surprise attack, captured the city.

Dale watched the events with interest, but from a distance. He had returned to farming near Fort Mims and supplied corn to Jackson's starving troops when they came back from Pensacola.

Later, the United States Army quartermaster refused to accept the frontiersman's claim. Dale went to Jackson. Old Hickory said nothing. He strode over to his table, scratched on a slip of paper with a crow-quill pen, dashed sand on the paper, and handed it to Dale.

The frontiersman told his biographer:

I was about to say something when he exclaimed, "Not a word, Major! Present that note."

He had written only three words: "Settle with Dale." In half an hour the money was in my pocket.

President Madison recognized the vital connection between the Creek War and the War of 1812. Addressing Congress, he said:

On our Southern border victory has continued to follow the American standard. The bold and skillful operations of Major General Jackson have subdued the principal tribes of hostile savages and, by establishing a peace with them, has best guarded against the mischief of their cooperation with the British enterprises which may be planned against that quarter of our country.

The British enterprise planned against the Southern quarter of the country was the seizure of the Mississippi Valley, with the city of New Orleans the primary objective. France's armies in Europe having been decisively defeated and Napoleon exiled to the island of Elba, England was at last free to send heavy contingents of fighting units to settle once and for all with the upstart Americans.

Peace commissioners from the United States had arrived in Ghent, Belgium, in the spring of 1814, hoping to sign an honorable treaty ending the War of 1812. The Crown's commissioners had kept them waiting a month, and when they finally did arrive, they treated the Americans as representatives of a defeated country. Through the summer and the fall and the winter, the angry Americans kept rejecting the disgraceful terms that the English tried to force upon them.

The fact of the matter was that the English were stalling until they had received word of their expected triumph at New Orleans.

The 1814 attack on the east coast, in which the British had burned Washington, was actually a diversion. England's main operation was aimed at New Orleans. If they captured this city, the king's men would then ascend the Mississippi and join the 10,000 redcoats in Canada, thus permanently stunting the growth of the ex-colony.

As remote a spot as it was in relation to the rest of the country, New Orleans was the most strategically located city in the United States. Above it were the developing areas of Louisiana, the Mississippi Territory, Missouri, Tennessee, Kentucky, and Illinois. As the frontiersmen hacked their way through the great forest that covered the entire eastern part of the nation they sent their produce down the streams and rivers running into the Mississippi—America's jugular—to New Orleans, and from there to the rest of the world. In the same way the manufactured goods that frontiersmen needed so badly came to them through New Orleans from other countries.

New Orleans, whose population was about 18,000, was a city of mixed blood—French, Spanish, German, English, American, Irish, Italian, Dutch, Negro, mulatto, quadroon, octoroon. Crown intelligence experts theorized that these people had little loyalty to the United States. Most of them didn't even speak English or the American version of it.

The British estimated that the city's warehouses contained about fifteen million dollars worth of cotton, sugar, flour, whisky, hides, and other produce from the Western and Southern frontier. (American estimates ran much higher.) The British slogan for the operation was Booty and Beauty.

On December 10, 1814, a Crown fleet of fifty sail dropped anchor off Ship Island about forty miles from New Orleans in the Gulf of Mexico. Aboard were eight thousand seasoned troops, including four regiments of the army that had burned Washington, a brigade of the Duke of Wellington's veterans from the bitter fighting in Spain, and the Ninety-Third Highlanders.

At dusk on December 22 the British advance guard, guided by Spanish fishermen, appeared in small boats off the mouth of Bayou Bienvenue, a turbid waterway

that wound from Lake Borgne through dense canebrake and cypress swamp to the rear entrance of New
Orleans. The British were about thirteen miles as the
crow flies from the Place d'Armes, the heart of the
American city. The route was not obstructed by fallen
trees and was lightly guarded. The last European invasion of the United States had begun.

Dale, however, as well as most of his countrymen,
knew nothing of the military situation. On New Year's
Eve of 1814 he was in the Creek Agency at Milledgeville, Georgia, ringing in the new year with his old
friend, Colonel Hawkins. Late that night an express
rider arrived with mail from Secretary of War James
Monroe for General Jackson, believed to be somewhere around New Orleans, preparing its defense
against the expected British invasion.

The dispatches were urgent, but clearly the horse
and its rider were in no condition to continue the
journey. Colonel Hawkins urged Dale to take over the
assignment. The route lay through more than five
hundred miles of dense wilderness, much of it Creek
country. Although the Indians and the settlers were
officially at peace, Dale knew perfectly well that
there were many disgruntled warriors who would be
overjoyed at the opportunity to lift his hair.

Nevertheless, Dale did not hesitate. At the Agency
he bought a horse named Paddy, a small, muscular
animal noted for his wind. With a blanket, a brace of
pistols, some ammunition, flint and steel to start fires,
and a wallet of parched corn for himself and his

mount, Dale set out for New Orleans shortly before daybreak on January 1, 1815.

Paddy's reputation for wind was well founded. He proved to be as tough as his rider. Traveling from dawn to midnight, fording streams, swimming rivers, they covered about eighty miles a day. The weather was wretched. Paddy and Dale pushed on through frigid, driving, nearly blinding rains laced with sleet that steamed off Paddy's glistening coat, but froze Dale's buckskins to his body.

On occasion the frontiersman found a cave in which they could spend the night. Sometimes he was able to build a lean-to that sheltered them both. But frequently he was forced to sleep in a tree, Paddy tethered below. More often than not, the wood was too wet for him to make a fire, and he and Paddy had to shiver out the night, waiting for the pallid, warmthless dawn and the resumption of their dour journey.

Astride his rugged little mount, Dale topped rise after rise in the white frost of early morning and saw beneath him a sea of trees emerald green in the pale sunlight, stretching as far as the eye could see and farther yet. He and Paddy skirted dismal, stinking swamps and rode through huge, clattering thickets of cane. If he encountered any wolves or hostile Indians, Dale neglected to mention them to his biographer. Much of the country he traversed was desolate. Were it not for the thick wallet of parched corn, horse and rider would have starved to death.

In seven and a half days Dale reached Madison-

ville, across Lake Pontchartrain from New Orleans.
He entrusted Paddy to a farmer, then chartered a fishing smack to take him across to the other shore. Its
waves whipped up by the winter winds, Lake Pontchartrain was more like an ocean.

After a whistling, jostling, drenching voyage that
took most of the night and made him wretchedly ill,
Dale staggered ashore at Fort Saint John. An old
Spanish fort with thick brick walls that bristled with
cannon, it was located at the mouth of Bayou Saint
John. Upon showing the dispatches there, Dale was
given a horse. At once he swung into the saddle, glad
to be back in his element. The express rider from
Mobile was also at the fort, but he was in no hurry.
Dale rode alone.

The road lay along Bayou Saint John, a narrow,
winding stream that ran through dense woods and
swamp more or less in the direction of New Orleans.
By the time Dale reached the city, it was nearly
dawn. The day was Sunday, January 8, 1815.

Apprehension lay upon New Orleans almost as
tangibly as the clammy fog. Freshly reinforced, the
enemy was knocking at the back door with 10,000
well-armed veteran troops. They were led by Sir Michael Pakenham, the Duke of Wellington's brother-in-
law and an experienced soldier who was called the
Hero of Salamanca for his smashing victory against
Napoleon's troops in Spain. Second only to the Iron
Duke himself in popularity with the English, Pakenham was the beau ideal of the British fighting man,

thoroughly schooled in the art of warfare on the wet, red fields of Europe. His troops were part of the army that was considered the finest in the world. He was thirty-six years old and in vigorous health.

His opponent was forty-seven and so wracked by the dysentery incurred during the Creek War that he was forced to dictate most of his orders from his couch. Though a born fighter, Jackson possessed only a meager knowledge of military science. He had a poorly equipped army of about 4000 men, composed of two United States Army regiments and a detachment of marines, augmented by a motley force of Choctaw Indians, New Orleans dandies and other Creoles, Free Men of Color, seamen, Jean Lafitte's buccaneers, and raw militia from Kentucky, Tennessee, Louisiana, and the Mississippi Territory.

The majority of Jackson's troops were made up of the militia—frontiersmen who, like their ailing leader, had gained all their combat experience fighting Indians in the Southern forest. Wearing their coonskin cap, grimy buckskins, and homespun hunting shirt, and with their almost complete lack of discipline, they looked like sorry soldiers. But they knew how vital the Mississippi River and New Orleans were to them, and they had readily responded to Jackson's frenzied appeals for fighting men.

On January 4 more than 2000 frontiersmen had arrived from Kentucky. Only 550 of them, however, were armed. Desperately Jackson had ransacked the homes of New Orleans for fowling pieces and muskets —anything that would shoot. Many of the Kentuckians were in rags. Jackson put the women of the city to work making clothes for his men.

Old Hickory had used up all his ammunition and most of his flints during the Creek War. Jean Lafitte, the patriotic and wealthy buccaneer, thereupon turned over his well-stocked magazine to the Americans and also furnished all of Old Hickory's cannon.

The English were contemptuous of the Americans, whom they called Dirty Shirts. So supremely confident were the invaders of victory that Pakenham carried a commission as governor of Louisiana with him.

Jackson had put New Orleans under martial law. No one was permitted to leave the city. Streetlamps were extinguished at 9 P.M. Any civilian found on the streets after curfew was arrested as a spy. The rumor was that Jackson planned to follow the example of the Russians at Moscow and destroy New Orleans rather than let the city and its rich stores fall into the hands of the enemy. Reportedly, a ship had been loaded with gunpowder for this purpose and was standing by in the event that the English broke the American line. Certain members of the state legislature had met, preparing to make terms with the enemy to prevent New Orleans from being blown up.

Such were the circumstances when Sam Dale came splashing through the muddy streets of the city just before dawn on January 8. Shouting to the guards posted on the corners for directions, he made his way to Jackson's headquarters. They were located in a three-story brick building with a black iron balcony at 106 Rue Royal. Overhead the Stars and Stripes drooped in the fog.

Dale jumped off his horse, gave the reins to a guard to hold, and rushed inside with the dispatches, calling for Jackson. Jackson wasn't there. He was with his troops on the plains of Chalmette about five miles below the city, a red-eyed staff officer told Dale, awaiting the expected British attack.

Grabbing up a rifle, Dale ran out, vaulted onto his horse, and galloped through the sleeping city, past the dark towers of Saint Louis Cathedral, past the empty square of the Place d'Armes. On his right the Mississippi River was a limbo of swirling gray fog in the dead light that preceded daybreak.

After a gallop of about two miles along the river road, he passed a low breastwork—Jackson's last line of defense. About two miles farther downriver he passed another breastwork, Jackson's second line of defense. The empty mud walls had an ominous air. Obviously prepared for the worst, Jackson was determined to make the British pay dearly for any American territory that they might occupy.

By this time the day had dawned. In the thick gray pall dead ahead, the sun looked like the moon. Over his horse's hoofbeats Dale could hear a thudding muffled by distance and the muggy air—cannon fire. The frontiersman urged his mount forward at its top speed, the distant thuds becoming steadily sharper and more frequent, rainbow flashes of light appearing in the mist. Then Dale heard another sound—music. A band was playing. At first he couldn't make out the tune, but as his horse carried him closer to the American line, he finally identified it. The band was playing "Yankee Doodle."

Jackson's first line of defense was a rampart of fence posts, logs, boards, cotton bales, and mud, between five and seven feet high, which stretched about 700 yards from the river to an impassable cypress swamp. The wall was directly behind Rodriguez Canal, an abandoned millrace ranging from ten to twenty feet wide and from four to eight feet deep. Jackson had cut the levee to flood the canal, but the river had fallen and the water in the canal was shallow.

At intervals along the rampart Jackson had emplaced eight batteries of artillery to support his riflemen. Against a frontal assault, the position was strong, about as strong as it could be under the circumstances, and a frontal assault—with certain variations—was the British battle plan.

On January 8, Pakenham's total attacking force numbered about 8000. Opposing him were about 3200 men—many of whom were unarmed, as an American deserter readily informed his British interrogators. Another 800 under Commodore Daniel T. Patterson guarded the approach to New Orleans on the west bank of the river.

The British made the deserter point out to them the

part of Jackson's line that was held by the militia. This sector was just to the American right of Battery Number Seven, about in the middle of the earthworks. It was manned by 1400 of General William Carroll's Tennessee Volunteers and backed up by 520 Kentuckians under General John Adair.

Having defeated Europe's best, the English had no doubt whatever that they would encounter only niggling trouble with a wretched pack of Dirty Shirts. The undisciplined Americans would break and run at the sight of naked British steel, as they had done so often in the past.

Pakenham had earned his nickname by smashing through the French center at Salamanca. He planned to do the same at Chalmette, and so split his assault force into three groups. The first was made up of 1400 men under the very able Colonel William Thornton, who had decisively defeated the Americans at Bladensburg, Maryland, before burning Washington. Thornton was ordered to take his men across the Mississippi River in rowboats under cover of night, overwhelm Patterson's position, and then turn the captured guns on Jackson's line across the river.

When this tactic had been accomplished, the second group, under Major General John Keane and numbering 1200 men, would make a demonstration in force on Jackson's right flank by the river, drawing the fire of his heaviest batteries there. While the Americans were distracted by this feint, Pakenham would launch his main assault.

The third group, 2200 troops under Major General Samuel Gibbs, was to have the honor of storming the enemy center, a half mile away across the stubble of a sugarcane field.

The British main concern (which wasn't really much of one) was the enemy artillery in the assault area. Battery Number Six consisted of one gun, a twelve-pounder. Battery Number Seven had two cannon—a brass eighteen-pound culverin and a six-pounder. Battery Number Eight was a small brass carronade with a faulty carriage, and it was rather ineffective.

To cross the open field in quick time, even loaded down with their pack and other gear, should take the men only a few minutes. Combat-hardened troops that they were, they hardly would be fazed by the artillery fire. They could expect to take casualties of course, but British soldiers, they of the Bulldog Breed, were accustomed to taking casualties and going on to victory. In addition, early morning darkness and heavy fog would be all to their advantage and to the disadvantage of the American cannoneers. The small-arms fire of the Dirty Shirts worried them not at all.

The Forty-Fourth East Essex Infantry, under Lieutenant Colonel Thomas Mullins, would lead the main attack, carrying fascines, or bundles, of cane stalks, to throw into Rodriguez Canal for the troops to charge over, and ladders for scaling the mud wall. A regiment of West Indian Negroes would support Gibbs's right, keeping the enemy in that sector from coming to the aid of the assailed militia. Major General John Lambert would be in the rear center with two regiments of reserve. Freshly shaved, their uniforms cleaned, brass polished for the triumphant march into New Orleans, the British were confident that they would sleep Sunday night in city beds.

As for Jackson's battle plan, he had none other than to let the British attack him. Speaking of his Kentuckians, General Adair could have been referring to the frontiersmen in general when he told Old Hickory:

> My troops will fight behind breastworks or in the woods, but do not hazard an attack of raw militia in the open plain; they cannot be relied on. The officers are inexperienced, the soldiers without subordination or discipline. You would hazard too much by making an attack with them in the open plain against well-disciplined troops.

And Jackson knew he was all too right.

For success, Pakenham's battle plan depended upon all the troops getting into the proper position at the proper time—always a problem with military operations. Saturday night, January 7, Colonel Thornton's redcoats had encountered great difficulty getting across the Mississippi to the west bank, and the four-knot current carried their boats farther downstream than anticipated. As a result, the troops were not in position when they were supposed to be and could not start the battle, as intended.

A general with a cooler head would have seen the

serious interruption that this delay made in his plan and drawn up a new one. But Pakenham, the Hero of Salamanca, was a headstrong, gallant, and somewhat reckless man, who was convinced that courage and fortitude spelled success on any battlefield of the world. The British would just have to take more casualties.

In the foggy dark shortly before dawn Sunday, January 8, Keane's troops had taken their position near the river a quarter mile from the American right flank. Gibbs's men had lined up in front of a cypress forest a half mile across the cane field from the American center.

Then, almost at the point of execution, Pakenham learned that Mullins's men of the Forty-fourth, who were to lead the main assault, had failed to bring up the ladders and fascines. Furious, the general sent the men back to get them.

At about 6 A.M. the fog began to lift like a tattered white curtain, revealing the two columns of tightly packed redcoats. Signal rockets arched up, sputtering, glowing fuzzily in the mist; bugles blared the attack; the British surged forward; Jackson's cannoneers opened fire; and the American band struck up "Yankee Doodle."

12

THE
BATTLE
OF
NEW
ORLEANS

When Sam Dale galloped up to the rear of the American line, the battle was still just getting under way. Although the deafening clamor of the cannons was making his mount skittish, the frontiersman raced along behind the ramparts, searching for Jackson in the thick dun cannon smoke. He soon realized that to find the general in such wild confusion was impossible. The delivery of the dispatches would have to wait for a quieter time. He gave his horse to an orderly and, rifle in hand, rushed to the barricade. With the instinct of a born fighter, he chose the point in the line that was the most threatened.

The militia were standing three deep behind the rampart. Taking a mouthful of rifle balls, Dale pressed forward to the first rank. The cannonade from both sides reverberated in the heavy moist air, shaking the ground under him, the many-hued gun flashes

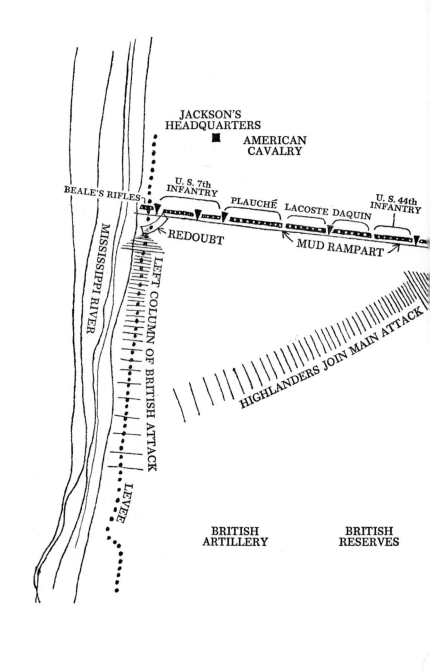

JACKSON'S
HEADQUARTERS

AMERICAN
CAVALRY

BEALE'S RIFLES

U. S. 7th
INFANTRY

PLAUCHÉ

LACOSTE DAQUIN

U. S. 44th
INFANTRY

REDOUBT

MUD RAMPART

MISSISSIPPI RIVER

LEFT COLUMN OF BRITISH ATTACK

HIGHLANDERS JOIN MAIN ATTACK

LEVEE

BRITISH
ARTILLERY

BRITISH
RESERVES

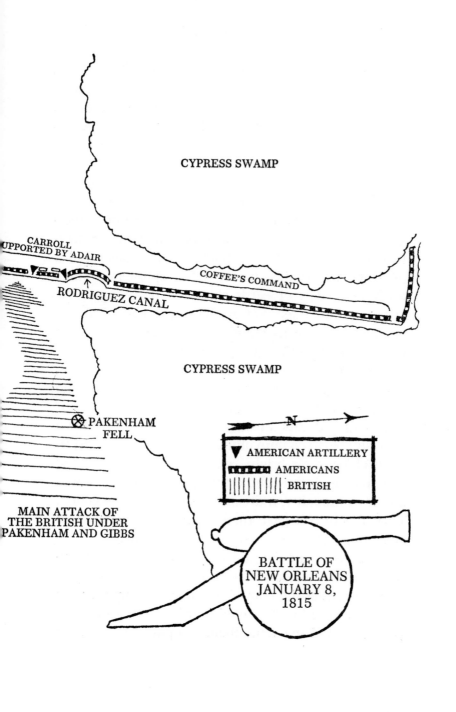

CYPRESS SWAMP

CARROLL
SUPPORTED BY ADAIR

COFFEE'S COMMAND

RODRIGUEZ CANAL

CYPRESS SWAMP

PAKENHAM
FELL

N

▼ AMERICAN ARTILLERY
███████ AMERICANS
|||||||||| BRITISH

MAIN ATTACK OF
THE BRITISH UNDER
PAKENHAM AND GIBBS

BATTLE OF
NEW ORLEANS
JANUARY 8,
1815

beautiful in the mist. The band, from the Orleans Battalion, struck up the "Marseillaise." It continued to play national and military airs throughout the action to cheer Jackson's troops—the first time that an American force had such a concert for an entire battle.

A fiery swoosh and a miniature comet came out of the eastern sky, tearing up the ground before the canal—a Congreve rocket. Sputtering and smoking, the iron cylinder filled with gunpowder came slithering through the grass like a serpent toward the nervous frontiersmen, then exploded with a flash and a great puff of white smoke. Metal splinters whined away and clods of earth showered down upon the cringing militiamen. Before the smoke had lifted, another rocket with its red glare and wild scream came over, and one continued to follow another.

"Mere toys to amuse children," Jackson called them, but they were disconcerting to the frontiersmen, who had never seen anything like them.

Gibbs's redcoats hustled across the dewy brown cane stubble in column of attack, sixty men abreast in close order, their bright red coats vivid against the gloom of the forest behind them. In the fog there was an air of unreality, a dreamlike quality to the action. Then the British gave three cheers and came on in quick time. They were about 500 yards away.

On Dale's right the gun captains at Battery Number Seven sighted down the barrel; struck a sharp pick into the vent at the rear of the tube, tearing open the bag of powder inside; salted powder from their flask in and around the vent; then, stepping back, fired a pistol at it. The flash ignited the powder in the vent; fire shot down to the bag in the tube. The cannons gave an earsplitting bark. There was a bright orange flash and a blossom of thick, white smoke as the guns rolled back on their recoil. The sweaty gunners pushed them up to the line again and sighted anew as the cannon balls hummed over the plain. Crashing into the British, the balls blasted big holes in their ranks, tossing men high into the air.

"I reckon those cannon are makin' a considerable noise," a frontiersman remarked.

"They're the noisiest kind of varmits to have for neighbors," a second answered.

The redcoats, coats redder yet from the blood of their fallen buddies, closed up and continued to come across the cane stubble with fixed bayonet and the earnest—and well-founded—conviction that nothing could withstand cold British steel. Canister exploded over them in a pretty puff of smoke and a hail of lead balls. Flights of grape went fluttering toward them "like flocks of partridges." The column shook and oscillated like a red ship upon a heavy sea. The head vanished. The flanks were thinned. The British closed up. Shorter, narrower, the column advanced in good order. It was about 300 yards off, within maximum range of the American long rifle, but the tense frontiersmen were ordered to hold their fire.

Dale said:

It was a magnificent vision. On each side our men stood silent and resolute. The enemy were ad-

vancing in columns, with loud cheers. Their martial approach to the American lines—the fearful
recoil, as whole detachments were swept away, the
heroism of their officers who rushed to the front,
waving their swords, and rallied their men into the
very jaws of death, and, cheering, died—was a
spectacle so sublime, that it silenced for a moment
the clamor of the battlefield, and inspired every
one with awe and admiration. There was a simultan-
eous pause in our ranks; a dreadful stillness pre-
vailed; not a gun was discharged; not a shout was
heard. . . .

Then all down the line sounded the dire *click-
clock, click-clock* as the militia rifles were cocked. The
redcoats were about 250 yards off.

Dale and the other frontiersmen, the best shots in
the world with the best rifle in the world, each slowly
raised his weapon. The long octagonal barrel held
true as the marksmen picked out individual targets in
the advancing column, the brass front sight lining up
with the V of the rear sight, zeroing in on the forehead or chest of a cheering British soldier.

The range was 200 yards. General Carroll yelled,
"Fire!"

All along the rampart the rifles released their sharp
thunder and orange lightning. A long thick roll of
reeking sulphurous smoke hung in the air and prevented the marksmen from seeing the results of their
fire. But they didn't have to see. They knew.

The British staggered back, hit much harder than

they had been by the cannon fire. But they were Englishmen, the Bulldog Breed. They closed up again and still came hustling over the canefield, cheering hoarsely, holding their gleaming British steel, toward the Dirty Shirts whom they held in such contempt.

"First rank, step down!" an American officer shouted. "Next rank forward!" Dale's line withdrew to load, and another line of marksmen took their place at the mud wall.

"Aim above the crossbelts!" the officer shouted. "Fire!"

The frontiersmen, who thought nothing of plunking a ball into the head of a squirrel at the top of the tallest tree, did not have to be told how to aim a weapon. Some did as ordered, sighting above the white X of the belts crossing the red enemy chests, but many aimed at the head.

About every ten seconds another lethal volley crashed out from the American ramparts. A witness described the steady rifle fusillades as "that constant rolling fire, whose tremendous noise resembled rattling peals of thunder." A British officer who survived wrote that the militia line looked like a long row of blazing furnaces. Both Americans and British said they had never seen such rapid fire.

"Never before had British veterans quailed," an English lieutenant wrote. "But it would be silly to deny that they did so now. That leaden torrent no man on earth could face."

The English troops, those who could, broke and ran. They ran all the way back to the forest and dived into a ditch, where at last they were safe from the galling, ghastly American fire. As the smoke rolled off the field all that could be seen in front of the mud wall were still red-coated bodies.

Gibbs tried without success to rally his men. Almost in tears, he galloped to Pakenham, crying, "The troops will not obey me! They will not follow me!"

But he spoke too soon. The troops were combat veterans, and they were British. Throwing off their heavy packs, they rallied. With Gibbs leading them on his horse, they charged forward, cheering, and were annihilated. Twenty yards from Rodriguez Canal, Gibbs fell, mortally wounded. A few of his men, a very few, splashed through the canal and clambered up the slippery side of the rampart, only to be killed or captured.

Pakenham dispatched an order to General Lambert to commit the reserve, then galloped forward about forty yards, waving his hat at his troops and shouting, "Remember, you're British!" A ball went through his thigh and killed his horse. Pakenham dragged himself upon another mount and started forward. Almost instantly a ball struck him in the neck, and then another in the groin. He was carried to the rear, eyes glazed, dying.

General Keane's column, as ordered, was making a demonstration in force upon Jackson's extreme right flank. Covered by the fog, which lasted longer by the river, the advance British companies, led by Colonel Robert Rennie, stormed a redoubt in front of the main American line. So quickly did the redcoats appear out of the fog that the Americans could fire only two volleys before the enemy was upon them.

In a sharp hand-to-hand fight, cold British steel drove out the redoubt's defenders. Climbing up on the breastwork, Rennie shouted, "Cease firing, you Yankee rascals!" To his men he cried, "The enemy's works are ours!"

A sharpshooter from Beale's Rifles, a crack Louisiana militia unit, put a ball into his forehead. Rennie and those of his men who had followed him up on the breastwork rolled like logs down the embankment as the militia fire dropped them. Rallying, the Americans counterattacked and won back the redoubt.

If the rest of the redcoats had followed their advance companies, they might have won the day for British arms—and the history of the world might have been different. But the methodical Keane was obeying orders, making only a feint. He held his main column back, anxiously studying the explosive action at the American center. When he saw Gibbs's troops faltering, he ordered the Ninety-third Highlanders to support them.

The Scot commander, Colonel Robert Dale, handed his watch and a letter to a surgeon. "Give these to my wife," he said. "I shall die at the head of my regiment."

To reach the American center, the Ninety-third had to pass Jackson's entire right flank, taking its terrible fire all the way. The Highlanders (forty years later "the thin red line" at Balaclava in the Crimean War) were all at least six feet tall, lean, angular, stern-faced men, who had taken fire on many battlefields of the world. But they had never taken such fire as they took on the dewy plain of Chalmette.

After a short, bloody march, they reached the American center, wheeled into a front of one hundred men, and charged forward. Fluttering grape tore big, raw holes in their ranks; buzzing rifle balls dropped them one by one. They heard a *thunk, thunk, thunk,* and all around them their chums were struck down. But they were Scots. They closed up and came on. Kilts swinging, they advanced across the incarmined cane stubble, stepping around, stumbling and jumping over the bodies of their predecessors. Grim and white-faced, they were driven by their ancient Celtic pride, the measured beat of their drums, and the wild, weird, howling, screaming, skirling of the bagpipes playing their tunes of glory, prodding them to death and glory.

"Fire! Load! Aim! Fire!" The gray winter morning was thick with American lead as the steady, endless, relentless volleys of rifle fire sounded. Allegedly, the officers' voices quavered as they gave their commands, and tears cut little trails on the powder-blackened faces of many frontiersmen. Still the British came on, and still the Americans fired.

Colonel Robert Dale died at the head of his regiment. Keane led the regiments on and fell with a rifle ball in the neck, 150 yards from the militia ramparts. Leaderless, the Scots milled around in disorder, drums quiet, pipes trailing off into silence. Other units charged up and rammed into the halted troops, breeding confusion, then panic.

A Major Wilkinson of the Twenty-first Royal North British Fusiliers rushed forward, waving his sword. Maybe a hundred of his redcoats followed. Maybe sixty of them reached Rodriguez Canal. Splashing through the water, slipping and sliding on the sloppy mud wall, twenty may have reached the breastworks, where they all were killed or captured.

As his head and shoulders came up to the parapet, Wilkinson was riddled. But he forced himself up, then collapsed across the top. He was carried to the rear of the American line. "Bear up, my dear fellow," a Major Smiley of the Kentuckians told him. "You're too brave a man to die."

"I thank you from my heart," the young officer murmured. "It's all over with me. You can render me a favor. It's to communicate to my commander that I fell on your parapet and died like a soldier and a true Englishman." He died two hours later; his commander was already dead.

The shocked British troops saw their three commanding officers, Pakenham, Gibbs, and Keane, all being carried off the field at the same time. Losing heart completely, the survivors fell back.

Pakenham's last command had been to throw in the reserve. A disciplined soldier, General Lambert ordered the buglar to sound the advance. As the youth raised the instrument to his lips, a bullet ripped through his right arm, and the bugle fell to the

ground. American rifle balls were buzzing among the redcoats like wasps, and all around Lambert men were dropping. Given that moment for reflection, the general decided not to carry out his orders. He acted out of intelligence rather than cowardice. Less than five months later he commanded a brigade at Waterloo and was singled out in Wellington's dispatches as having "conducted the movement of his brigade in a most able manner."

"Cease firing! Cease firing!" The call ran down the line.

The sounds of battle died to a humming silence. The ground before the American ramparts was thickly dotted with thousands upon thousands of little greased leather patches. As the white smoke slowly and majestically rolled off the plain, the frontiersmen witnessed an awesome sight. In front of their sector, stretching back two hundred yards and more, the field resembled a lake of blood. So thickly strewn were the redcoat dead and wounded that one could have walked a quarter mile out from the American lines without setting foot on the ground.

The course of the British across the field could be traced clearly in the thick red line of their casualties. In some places whole platoons lay together, apparently killed by the same volley.

A contemporary historian observed:

Dressed in their gay uniforms, cleanly shaved and attired for the promised victory and triumphal entry into the city, these stalwart men lay on the gory field, frightful examples of the horrors of war. Strangely indeed did they contrast with those ragged, unshorn, begrimed, and untidy, strange-looking, long-haired men, who, crowding the American parapet, coolly surveyed the terrible destruction they had caused.

As Dale told his biographer:

The terrible grandeur of the scene impressed the veteran soldiers of Napoleon, a number of whom were in the American ranks, and you may imagine its effect upon me, trained from boyhood to the ambuscades of the wilderness, and to the hand-to-hand rencounters of the frontier, where a reeking scalp is often the only evidence of the fight.

Dale could have been speaking for all Southern frontiersmen, who had shared many of his earlier experiences, but who had never seen anything like the red-carpeted plain of Chalmette on that cold Sunday morning of January 8, 1815.

Accompanied by his staff, Jackson rode slowly down the rear of the American ramparts, halting at each command to praise the officers and men. As he passed the band, it struck up "Hail Columbia," and the entire American army broke into wild cheers.

In about twenty minutes the British had taken some 2000 casualties. Estimates of their losses vary: one of their reports gave 1971 killed and wounded. The official American estimate of the enemy loss was 2600. Other estimates ran to 3000 or more. According to the official regimental history, the Fourth (King's Own) Regiment lost over 400 men—more than three times their losses at Waterloo. The Twenty-first took 500 casualties. The Ninety-third Highlanders, according to the adjutant, had 900 men and 25 officers the morning of January 8. After the battle, he said, the regiment mustered 130 men and 9 officers. To show the incredible accuracy of the frontiersmen's rifle fire, British casualties included 1 lieutenant general, 2 major generals, 8 colonels, and lieutenant colonels, 6 majors, 18 captains, and 54 lieutenants.

The Battle of New Orleans was one of the most stunning and one-sided defeats in the history of the British Empire.

The American small-arms fire died out about 8:30 A.M. The batteries banged away until 2 P.M. But the outcome was decided once and for all in that first murderous twenty minutes. When finally the last echo of the last cannon shot had died, more than 500 able-bodied British troops rose up from among their dead and wounded comrades and came forward with their hands up. Some of these redcoats who had feigned death ran back to rejoin their outfit. One, when he thought he was out of rifle shot, began to thumb his nose at the Americans. A score of frontiersmen took a shot at him, but the distance was too great; the bullets kicked up the dirt well in front of him. Emboldened, the redcoat began to make more insulting gestures.

A militia officer called up one of his men, a pallid,

cadaverous Tennessean nicknamed Paleface, a famed sharpshooter. Deliberately Paleface screwed a fresh flint into the hammer of his rifle, measured out the precise amount of powder he judged necessary, poured it down the barrel, selected the most symmetrical ball in his shot bag, centered in on an oiled patch, and rammed it home. Resting the rifle on the rampart, Paleface put his sunken cheek to the stock, ran his sight along the distant target, and, allowing for wind and distance, touched the trigger.

With a final contemptuous gesture, the British soldier had turned to rejoin his company. He had taken a couple of steps when he fell flat on his face. The Americans cheered. Paleface got permission from his commanding officer to walk off the distance. He found it to be more than 300 long paces to the dead soldier. The ball had hit the man square between the shoulder blades.

An English officer refused to surrender to one of the militia and was walking off when the frontiersman drew a bead on him and yelled, "Halt, Mr. Redcoat. One more step and I'll blow a hole through your hide!"

Angrily, the redcoat halted and turned with hands upraised, exclaiming, "What a disgrace for a British officer to have to surrender to a chimney sweep!"

That remark summed up the British attitude. They still had nothing but contempt for the Dirty Shirts. Outraged, they accused the American deserter of directing their attack at the part of the line held by the best-trained regulars in the United States Army and marched him to a tall cypress. There he protested his innocence until a rope choked off his words.

Jackson detailed men to help the enemy gather up their killed and wounded. A Tennessean assigned to this grisly chore gazed down upon the body of an Englishman, noting that two bullets had gone through his head. One had struck him over the left eye and passed out behind the right ear. The other had hit him below the right eye and come out above the left ear. Either would have been instantly fatal.

"A little lead wasted there," was the frontiersman's laconic comment.

The English officer George Robert Gleig wrote:

Of all the sights I ever witnessed that which met me (on the field) was beyond comparison the most shocking and the most humiliating. Within the small compass of a few hundred yards were gathered together nearly a thousand bodies, all of them arrayed in British uniforms.

Not a single American was among them; all were English; and they were thrown by dozens into shallow holes, scarcely deep enough to furnish them with a slight covering of earth. Nor was this all. An American officer stood by smoking a segar, and apparently counting the slain with a look of savage exultation; and repeating over and over to each individual that approached him, that their loss came to only eight men killed and fourteen wounded.

*   *   *

Actually, the cigar-smoking officer's report was a trifle high. Difficult as the statistics are to believe, the American casualties behind Rodriguez Canal were only seven killed and six wounded.

The British tried to blame the loss of the battle upon the death of Pakenham and also upon the incompetent Mullins, who was later court-martialed and dismissed from the army. But the real reason had nothing to do with either of these men. It was well expressed by Marshal Count Bertrand Clausel, the Frenchman whose division Pakenham had routed at Salamanca.

Visiting Chalmette five years after the battle, he was puzzled how such a comparatively weak force could smash such a strong body of fine troops. Then he cried, "Ah! I see how it all happened. When these Americans go into battle they forget that they're not shooting turkeys and try never to waste a shot!"

The Battle of New Orleans is one of the most brilliant defensive triumphs in history. It was as important to the United States as Saratoga, the victory that secured the alliance of France and led to the successful completion of the Revolutionary War, and Gettysburg, the battle that assured Union victory in the Civil War. Since the Treaty of Ghent had been signed on December 24, 1814, more than two weeks before, historians have called the battle a needless one. Nothing could be farther from the truth. The treaty specifically provided that it should not be effective until both the United States and Great Britain had ratified it. There can be no doubt that the British would have refused to ratify the treaty if their arms had been triumphant.

Probably the greatest significance of the Battle of New Orleans was in its effect upon political thinking. From the end of the Revolutionary War in 1783 until 1815, the United States had been in grave peril of splitting up into a series of small countries. Few men —American or European—thought the nation could endure. Many Americans considered themselves primarily citizens of their state rather than of the United States.

The English writer Dean Tucker observed:

As to the future grandeur of America, and its being a rising empire under one head, it is one of the idlest and most visionary notions that ever was conceived, even by writers of romance. When those immense regions beyond the back settlements are taken into account, they form the highest probability that the Americans never can be united into one compact empire under any species of government whatever. Their fate seems to be—a disunited people till the end of time.

The great American historian Henry Brooks Adams wrote of the United States of this period:

No prudent person dared to act on the certainty

that when settled, government could comprehend the whole; and when the day of separation should arrive, and America should have her Prussia, Austria and Italy, as she already had her England, France and Spain, what else could follow but a return to the old conditions of local jealousies, wars and corruptions, which had made a slaughterhouse of Europe?

The Battle of New Orleans changed that prospect. The victory caused a great wave of national spirit and stimulated unification. Americans were stunned, then elated at the news. In Washington the *National Intelligencer* summed up the situation neatly with the huge headline:

ALMOST INCREDIBLE VICTORY! ! !

The era of colonialism that had lasted since 1607 had come to an end. When the body of Sir Michael Pakenham, "Governor of Louisiana," left for England in a cask of rum, it symbolized the new status quo. Henceforward, Europe kept hands off America. Much more blood would be spilled, but the conclusion was foregone as the American frontiersmen pressed their relentless march across the great plains, deserts, and mountains of the continent to the Pacific Ocean. At the Battle of New Orleans, the West was truly won.

Another final and far-reaching result was that Andrew Jackson rode off the plain of Chalmette as his nation's hero. For the first time a man of the Western border country arose to challenge the Easterners, who had, up to then, dominated the national politics of the United States.

All was not glory for American arms, however, on January 8, 1815. Across the river the militia broke and ran just as the British had expected them to. If the redcoats had pushed their advantage, they in all probability would have captured New Orleans. But General Lambert thought that his force on the east bank was too hurt and demoralized to follow through. He ordered his units across the river to withdraw, and the Union Jack did not fly over Louisiana.

13

THE RIDE BACK

Dale was unable to deliver the dispatches to Andrew Jackson until late Sunday night. He found the general in his field headquarters at the Macarty plantation house behind the right flank of the American line. Jackson had returned there after the battle. Among those waiting to see him was the express rider from Mobile, who had finally arrived.

Jackson was sitting at a desk in a book-lined room, rapidly dictating a series of orders for messengers who hovered close by, waiting to rush off with them. In the soft, wavering light of the whale-oil lamp, he looked exhausted and sick.

When his turn came, Dale stepped forward and presented his dispatches. Impatiently, Jackson tore the heavy envelopes open and glanced through their contents. With a snort of disgust, he tossed them on his desk. "Too late, too late!" he cried in his high, reedy voice. "They're always too late in Washington!"

What the dispatches were, Dale didn't say and probably didn't know. The incident would be highly dramatic if one of them had announced the Treaty of Ghent, but there is no such possibility. The report of the treaty did not reach Jackson until March 13, 1815, nearly a month after Congress had ratified it.

Dale congratulated Jackson on his victory. The general jumped up, shook the frontiersman's hand, and said, "Major, if those fellows on the other bank had done their duty, it would have been a glorious day!"

Old Hickory was six feet and one inch in height, an inch shorter than Dale, and he weighed fifty pounds less. He was clean-shaven with a wild mass of sandy hair beginning to gray. His deeply creased, sallow face still bore the white scar of an English saber cut received at the age of thirteen for refusing to black an enemy officer's boots. He had not been fond of the British since and must have derived enormous gratification from his smashing victory over them. Yet he treated the vanquished with honor and courtesy, even returning General Keane's sword, which the Englishman had dropped on the battlefield when he was wounded.

At Dale's request, one of Jackson's aides, a Major Chotard, told the general that, since there was little fighting in the Creek nation then, the frontiersman wanted to remain with the United States Army.

"Are you broken down by your ride?" Jackson asked politely enough, apparently thinking Dale wanted to avoid the return trip.

"No, sir," Dale answered. "But I desire to be with you."

Dale told his biographer:

Holding up the dispatches, Jackson turned to his officers and said, "This express has been brought from Georgia in *eight days*. From Mobile our expresses are often fourteen days on the route. Chotard, don't speak to me of stopping Major Dale. No, sir. You must return to the Agency and to Milledgeville as fast as you have come."

Old Hickory asked the frontiersman about the other commands and the disposition of the Indians. Dale tried to answer, but was repeatedly interrupted by the express rider from Mobile.

Dale reported:

Being thus annoyed several times, the general cried out, "D--n you, sir, be silent till I ask you a question!"

When he finished his inquiries, he faced the other and said, "Now, sir, what do you know?"

"Nothing more, sir. Major Dale has told you all."

"Yes, d--n you,," said the general. "I thought so. You are too slow a traveler to bring news. Chotard, write an order to Piatt to mount Major Dale on the best horse to be had."

At this point Dale broke in to ask what would be done with Paddy.

Jackson glanced up in annoyance. "Who the hell is Paddy, sir?"

"The pony, General, that I rode from Georgia."

Jackson's dark blue eyes widened in surprise. "You don't mean to say, sir, that you rode one horse all the way from Georgia in seven and a half days!"

"I mean nothing less, General."

"Then, sir, he won't be able to go back!"

For one of the few times in his life, Dale bragged a bit. "He is like myself, General—very tough."

Old Hickory took this answer into consideration. He, himself, knew something about toughness. "Tell me," he said, "how far can you ride on that horse in a day?"

"Seventy or eighty miles from daybreak to midnight with light weights."

"Light weights!"

"Yes, sir. An empty belly and no saddlebags."

Jackson turned back to his aide. "Chotard, give Major Dale my authority, should his horse fag, to ask any man he meets to dismount, and if he refuses to knock him off and seize his horse." He gave Dale a craggy grin. "And, Major, I know you'll do it!"

By then it was close on midnight. Dale ate for the first time that day and tasted meat for the first time since he had left Georgia. Finally, wrapping himself in his blanket, he stretched out on the floor by the fire. Unfazed by Old Hickory's high-pitched voice as he dictated the battle report, the weary frontiersman was soon fast asleep.

He set out at dawn next morning, accompanied by one of Jackson's staff officers. They rode north to the shore of Lake Pontchartrain, where Dale found another fishing smack to take him across. On the other side he reclaimed Paddy from the farmer.

The little horse was fresh and ready to go. Dale swung into the saddle and put Paddy into an easy, ground-covering canter. They had gone only a short distance when the frontiersman sighted a mounted American officer in the road ahead.

"Where're you from?" the officer demanded as Dale rode up.

"Headquarters," the frontiersman said, guiding Paddy around the other horse.

The officer moved to block him. "You must stop and tell me the news!"

Dale gave Paddy his heels and the little horse scooted ahead. "Can't stop," Dale said. "If you want the news you must travel my way."

"Sir, you don't know me!" the officer shouted. "I'm Colonel Sparks of the United States Army! You must stop!"

"And I, sir, am Major Sam Dale," the frontiersman called over his shoulder. "And when I'm under orders I stop for no man!"

Angrily but resignedly, the officer wheeled around his horse and rode with Dale for several miles, getting the news of the battle. Later it was reported to Dale that when the officer told Jackson of the incident Old Hickory cried, "There isn't a man this side of hell can stop Big Sam and, Sparks, if you *had* stopped him I'd have had you shot!"

The ride back was a grueling repeat of the trip to New Orleans. If anything, the weather was colder, wetter, more wretched than before. All the rivers and streams were swollen and swift. Dale crossed the Alabama in a pirogue at Random's Landing, the scene of the Canoe Battle, Paddy swimming behind.

Late the night of the fifth day, Dale and Paddy reached Fort Decatur on the Tallapoosa during a hard rain. The frontiersman later described the incident:

It was the coldest night I ever experienced, and my clothes were glued to my body. I was challenged by two sentinels who said I would have to report to the main guard, half a mile to the right, before I could be admitted into the lines.

I replied, "I should be dead before I could get there. I am freezing. Fire the alarm if you choose, but don't shoot me. You know me and my business!"

One of the guards ran forward to report to the commandant, who rushed out of his quarters, crying, "Light, Major Dale, light!" But the frontiersman was so done in that he could not dismount without aid. The commandant pushed Dale's right foot out of the stirrup and cocked his leg up and over the saddle.

The frontiersman watched him with remote interest, unable to help. He was as if glued to his mount.

The commandant ran around Paddy and pushed Dale's left foot out of the stirrup, then caught him as he fell. He threw his arm around the frontiersman, and, like two men in a three-legged race, they staggered though the driving rain into headquarters, as an orderly led Paddy to a warm, dry stable.

The commandant yelled for more wood for the fire. He made Dale drink a pint of hot coffee, well laced with whisky, then asked him for the news. Dale held out the sodden dispatch. The commandant took it and tossed it on the table. "You must tell it," he said.

So Dale told him the story of the battle. The veteran soldier listened intently, tears of pride and joy streaming down his face. When the frontiersman had finished, the commandant gave a great cheer.

"The officers came crowding in half-dressed," Dale said, "and then the men in masses around the door, and I was obliged to stand there and repeat the story until daylight."

At that point the commandant mercifully allowed him to sleep, putting a guard outside his door to prevent any latecomers from waking him up for a report of the battle.

Dale arrived in Milledgeville at sunset on the eighth day and delivered his dispatch. He had not found it necessary to commandeer another mount. Paddy had taken him the distance.

14

THE
END
OF
THE
FOREST

For some years after the war, Dale operated a general store in what is now Monroe County, Alabama. In 1816 he was elected a delegate to the convention called to divide the Mississippi Territory into the states of Mississippi and Alabama. The following year he was a delegate to Alabama's first General Assembly.

But Dale's Indian-fighting days were not yet over. On March 13, 1818, the families of William Ogle and Eli Stroude were massacred near Fort Claiborne. The assaults were led by the Creek chieftain Savannah Jack, whom Dale called "one of the bloodiest villains that ever infested any country."

Other attacks and ambushes followed. Dale raised thirty men and went after the hostiles. He chased them for months, but could never bring them to battle. Then suddenly the attacks quit. Hard-pressed, the Indians apparently had slipped across the Mississippi and were not heard from again. The Creeks had at last decided to leave the Americans in possession of the land that they had so reluctantly surrendered in 1814. New settlers flooded into the area, and the whack of the ax sounded unceasingly in the forest.

For eight terms Dale represented Monroe County in the state legislature. In 1821 Alabama conferred upon him the rank of brigadier general in the state militia.

In 1824 the Marquis de Lafayette made his last visit to the United States. Dale was a member of the committee that met the aging statesman at Alabama's eastern boundary and escorted him to the state capital. The Creeks had heard of the great exponent of liberty and gave him a warm welcome. When the long procession of horsemen and carriages came to Callabee Swamp, Dale found that the Indians had laid down a roadway of logs and were standing up to their shoulders in the water, holding the logs in place until everyone had passed.

"They then, at (Lafayette's) request, went through the exercises of the ball play," Dale said, "a display of strength and activity only to be seen among the Southern tribes, who by the way, are superior, physically and intellectually, more warlike, and capable of a higher civilization than any of the Northern or Western races."

During this period immigrants continued to pour

into Alabama and Mississippi. The new settlers had little or no food and hardly any money. They came to Dale at his store for supplies, trying to persuade him to extend them credit, begging him, even threatening him. The trade was not good business, but Big Sam was not a good businessman. He took his life savings of $4000 and bought flour and meat.

"These supplies," he said, "I distributed on twelve months' credit among thousands of people, many of them utter strangers to me, and it ended in my ruin." Because, of course, whatever they said at the time, whatever their intentions upon the teary occasion, few of his creditors bothered to repay him.

As more white men crowded into the area, the Indians had to relinquish more of their land. The Choctaw nation originally occupied about twenty-five million acres in the central and southern part of Mississippi and southwestern Alabama. In 1820 the Choctaws ceded fifteen million acres to the United States. On September 27, 1830, at the Treaty of Dancing Rabbit Creek, they ceded the other ten million acres.

In 1832 the Secretary of War appointed Colonel George S. Gaines and General Dale to supervise the removal of the Choctaws to their new home across the Mississippi River in what is now Oklahoma and Arkansas. From one of these Indians Dale bought some land outside the present town of Daleville in Lauderdale County, Mississippi, and later represented the county for a term in the state legislature.

Dale told his biographer:

I found the great body of the Choctaws very sad,
making no arrangements until the last moment to
remove, clinging around their humble cabins, and
returning again and again to the resting places of
their dead.

Even the sternest warriors, trained to suppress
every emotion, appeared unmanned, and, when we
camped at night, many of them stole back in the
darkness twenty, thirty, and even forty miles to
take a last fond look at the graves of their house-
hold, soon to be trampled upon by a more enter-
prising and less sentimental race.

While Dale was leading the Indians through the
forest, his horse stepped into a hole, fell, and rolled
over on him, badly dislocating the shoulder injured at
the Canoe Battle and inflicting severe internal in-
juries. Dale was still a fine specimen, but he was worn
down by his rugged life, and he was sixty years old.
At last he was forced to give up the emigration service.

He was also without funds. He decided to go to
Washington City and see about his claims of a large
amount of money due him from the Federal government for corn and other supplies that he had furnished the United States Army at various times.

Washington City was not beautiful. It had been
laid out by the French engineer, Major Pierre Charles
L'Enfant, in a neat geometric pattern intended to
make it the most attractive and impressive capital in

the world. In 1832, when Dale arrived, Washington hardly had earned this title. It had amazingly wide streets, some of them paved. It was crisscrossed by muddy ditches and dotted with malarial swamps and pine-scraggled hillocks. Those who could afford the expense rode in carriages; those who couldn't walked and got splattered.

The Capitol building, burned by the British in 1814, was not yet fully restored. Other structures that housed the State, Treasury, War, and Navy Departments were small, of brick, and quite unimpressive. Washington, as Dale soon learned, was a city of rumors, gossip, slander, and scandal.

The shy, retiring frontiersman was particularly impressed by its women:

> The ladies of Washington struck me, who had so long been accustomed to the sunburned maidens of the woods, as very fair and beautiful, very fascinating and refined. In one thing they differ from our Indian women: they look one full in the face, and it is difficult to withstand their glances. An Indian maid, when a warrior approaches, bends her head like a drooping leaf. . . .

Dale put up at Brown's Hotel. The name of Big Sam was well known, even in the nation's capital, and soon after his arrival a party was given for him at the hotel. One of the guests spoke lightly of the opposite sex, addressing his remarks directly to the frontiersman, apparently trying to impress him.

"Sir," Dale cried, jumping to his feet, "no man with a true heart sneers at women. No gentleman ever boasts of his gallantries!" Thereupon, he tossed his wine into the other man's face and stalked out of the room.

The braggart was said to be very belligerent, and the frontiersman expected to be challenged to a duel. No challenge came. He heard that the man had tried to laugh off the incident, saying that Dale was tight, but he never appeared in the frontiersman's presence again.

Day after day, Dale patiently carried his claim to Capitol Hill, cutting through the mesh of red tape that even then entangled the halls of government. He got past the first auditor. He got past the second. He came to the third and last.

Dale said:

Such a man I never saw before. The moment the word *claim* was mentioned, he stiffened his back, drew up his legs, pulled down his spectacles, pricked up his ears, and stuck out his mouth as though he would bite. I would rather encounter half a dozen Indians than such a harrier of a man. His integrity was unimpeachable, but he worried me much, and I left the matter unsettled.

Meanwhile, President Jackson had learned of his old friend's arrival and sent Senator William R. King of Alabama to bring Dale to him. "Tell Dale," Old Hickory instructed Colonel King, "that if I had as little to do as he has, I should have seen him before now."

Jackson did not know the real purpose of Dale's visit to Washington. Undoubtedly, if he had known, the President would have settled the claim as speedily as he had years earlier with his three-word message to the Army quartermaster. But Dale had been in Washington long enough to know that Jackson and his spoils system form of patronage was under severe criticism. If the President intervened on behalf of a crony, there could be serious political repercussions. Dale would do nothing to damage his old friend, however rightful his claim, however much he needed the money. He kept his silence and never did receive payment.

The Mansion, as the White House was then called, was at the opposite end of Pennsylvania Avenue from Capitol Hill. Dale and Colonel King rode a hackney up the tree-lined roadway, which the President had just had macadamized. Old Hickory was pacing the lawn in front of the south portico as the two men trudged up the new gravel walk. He was much grayer and even thinner than when Dale had last seen him in New Orleans seventeen years earlier. His sallow cheeks were sunken, and he looked very, very tired, but his eyes were as bright as ever. He rushed forward and seized Dale's hand in his firm grasp.

"No introduction is needed," Colonel King said.

"Oh, no," Jackson cried, shaking hands again. "I shall never forget Sam Dale!"

He led the frontiersman to the upstairs study.

There a group of politicians was in a heated discussion of nullification, the formal suspension by a state within its territorial jurisdiction of a Federal law: the States' Rights argument that has continued to be a bitterly contested issue into modern times.

"General Dale," Jackson cried in his reedy voice, "if this thing goes on, our country will be like a bag of meal with both ends open. Pick it up in the middle or endwise, and it will run out. I must tie the bag and save the country!"

When the others had left, Jackson and Dale each sat smoking his pipe in the study. "Sam," Old Hickory said, "you have been true to your country, but you have made one mistake in life. You're now old and solitary, without a bosom friend or family to comfort you. . . ."

He started to speak of his wife, Rachel, who had died in 1828, but his eyes filled with tears. He jumped up and began to stride up and down the room, trying to collect himself. "Dale," he said, pausing by a table, "they are trying me here. You will witness it. But, by the God of Heaven, I will uphold the laws!"

"I understood him to be referring to nullification again," Dale said. "I expressed the hope that things would go right."

"They *shall* go right, sir!" Old Hickory cried, slamming his fist on the table so hard that he broke his pipe.

Dale told his biographer:

When I rose to take leave, he pressed me to accept a room there. "I can talk to you at night. In the day I'm beset." I declined on the plea of business, but dined with him several times, always, no matter what dignitaries were present, sitting on his right hand. When we parted for the last time, he said, "My friend, farewell. We shall see each other no more. Let us meet in heaven."

I could only answer him with tears, for I felt that we should meet no more on earth.

Dale was right. Going home through Virginia and Georgia, he returned to the scenes of his early adventures. He visited the resting place of his parents, where he had spent a solitary vigil more than forty years earlier. The little graveyard was overgrown with briers and wild flowers and almost obliterated. He also met a few old friends, but most of those he had known were dead.

When he had last been in the area, it was Indian country—lonely, pathless wilderness haunted by danger yet glorious with the freedom of the wild. But now, wherever he looked, he saw towns, villages, roads, cultivated fields, and all the other appendages of civilization. The forest—the great, shadowy, green, cool, singing, aromatic, mystic forest—and everything that had made Big Sam Dale and those like him was gone and would never return.

He went on to his home outside Daleville, where he died alone at the age of sixty-nine on May 24, 1841. That night hundreds of miles away Jerry Austill, one of his comrades in the Canoe Battle, dreamed that a man he didn't know approached him, saying, "Dale is dead." Several days later a stranger came to him with the sad news.

BIBLIOGRAPHY

Bartram, William, *The Travels of William Bartram*. Philadelphia, 1791.

Bassett, John Spencer, *The Life of Andrew Jackson*. Garden City: Doubleday and Company, Inc., 1911.

Beirne, Francis F., *The War of 1812*. New York: E. P. Dutton and Company, Inc., 1949.

Brewer, W., *Alabama: Her History, Resources, War Record, and Public Men, From 1540 to 1872*. Montgomery: Barrett and Brown, 1872.

Brooks, Charles B., *The Siege of New Orleans*. Seattle: The University of Washington Press, 1961.

Bryant, Will, *Great American Guns and Frontier Fighters*. New York: Grosset and Dunlap, 1961.

Carter, Hodding, *Doomed Road of Empire, the Spanish Trail of Conquest*. New York: McGraw-Hill Book Company, 1963.

Claiborne, J. F. H., *The Life and Times of General Sam Dale, the Mississippi Partisan*. New York: Harper and Brothers, 1860.

——, *Mississippi as a Province, Territory and State*. Baton Rouge: Louisiana State University Press, reprinted 1964.

Coates, Robert M., *The Outlaw Years*. New York: The Macawlay Company, 1930.

De Grummond, Jane Lucas, *The Baratarians and the Battle of New Orleans*. Baton Rouge: Louisiana State University Press, 1961.

Dictionary of American Biography. New York: Charles Scribner's Sons, 1935.

Eaton, John Henry, *Memoirs of Andrew Jackson*. Philadelphia, 1833.

Halbert, A. S. and Ball, T. H., *The Creek War of 1813 and 1814*. Chicago: Donohue and Henneberry; Montgomery: White, Woodruff and Fowler, 1895.

Jones, George C., Jr., *Antiquities of the Southern Indians*. New York: D. Appelton and Company, 1873.

LaFarge, Oliver, *A Pictorial History of the American Indian*. New York: Crown Publishers, Inc., 1956.

Martin, Thomas M., *The Story of Horseshoe Bend National Military Park*. New York, San Francisco, Montreal: The Newcomen Society in North America, 1960.

Parton, James, *Life of Andrew Jackson*. New York: Mason Brothers, 1861.

Peterson, Harold L., *A History of Firearms*. New York: Charles Scribner's Sons, 1961.

Pickett, Albert James, *History of Alabama and Incidentally of Georgia and Mississippi from the Earliest Period*. Charleston: Walker and James, 1851.

Riley, B. F., *Makers and Romance of Alabama History*. Tuscaloosa, 1936.

Roush, J. Fred, *Chalmette National Historical Park, Louisiana*. Washington: National Park Service Historical Handbook Series No. 29, 1958.

Rowland, Dunbar, *Encyclopedia of Mississippi History*. Madison: Swlwyn A. Brant, 1907.

Simkins, Francis Butler, *A History of the South*. New York: Alfred A. Knopf, Inc., 1963.

Sloane, Eric, *Diary of an Early American Boy*. New York: Wilfred Funk, Inc., 1962.

Sutherland, John, *Men of Waterloo*. Englewood Cliffs: Prentice-Hall, Inc., 1966.

Van Every, Dale, *Ark of Empire, the American Frontier 1784-1803*. New York: William Morrow and Company, Inc., 1963.

——, *The Final Challenge, the American Frontier 1804-1845*. New York: William Morrow and Company, Inc., 1964.

Walker, Alexander, *Jackson and New Orleans*. Cincinnati: J. C. Derby, 1856.

INDEX

ABOUT THE AUTHOR . . .

JOHN FOSTER was born in Chicago and grew up in Oak Park, Illinois. After attending the University of Wisconsin briefly, he later gained a B.A. from Florida Southern College. He then took up graduate study in English and philosophy at the University of Florida. His career in journalism has included work on dailies in Lakeland, Florida, and Wilmington, North Carolina. He was assistant editor of *DIXIE* Roto, Sunday magazine of *The Times-Picayune*, in New Orleans, Louisiana, and is now editor of *Dawn*, weekend magazine of the *Suffolk Sun*, Deer Park, Long Island. In addition to his books for young people, he has written a novel for adults and a number of stories and articles that have appeared in this country, Canada, Great Britain, and Holland.

During World War II, Mr. Foster saw service as a Navy hospital corpsman with the Second Marine Division in the central Pacific and Japan. He has also traveled widely in the United States and Ireland. At present he and his wife and their two children live in Huntington, Long Island. An older daughter lives in New York City.